THE ZEN OF R2-D2

THE ZEN

of

R2-D2

ANCIENT WISDOM
from
A GALAXY FAR, FAR AWAY

Matthew Bortolin

Wisdom

Wisdom Publications
199 Elm Street
Somerville, MA 02144 USA
wisdomexperience.org

Library of Congress Cataloging-in-Publication Data
Names: Bortolin, Matthew, author.
Title: The Zen of R2-D2: ancient wisdom from a galaxy far, far away / Matthew Bortolin.
Description: Somerville: Wisdom Publications, 2019.
Identifiers: LCCN 2019014017 (print) | ISBN 9781614296201 (pbk.: alk. paper)
Subjects: LCSH: Zen Buddhism. | Star Wars films.
Classification: LCC BQ9265.6 .B67 2019 (print) | LCC BQ9265.6 (ebook) | DDC 294.3/927—dc23
LC record available at https://lccn.loc.gov/2019014017
LC ebook record available at https://lccn.loc.gov/2019980784

ISBN 978-1-61429-620-1   ebook ISBN 978-1-61429-621-8

23 22 21 20 19   5 4 3 2 1

Cover design by Phil Pascuzzo. Interior design by Kristin Goble.
Set in Adobe Garamond Pro 11.1/15.

Printed on acid-free paper and meets the guidelines for permanence and durability of the Production Guidelines for Book Longevity of the Council on Library Resources.

Printed in the United States of America.

For W, V, B, and H

CONTENTS

EPISODE I

MAKING NEW FRIENDS AT STAR WARS CELEBRATION

He's a foul-mouthed, greasy bucket of bolts, but there is no one in Star Wars that embodies the qualities of Zen like R2-D2.

I have barely finished typing these words on my laptop when a familiar golden protocol droid shuffles up to me and says in a lilting British accent, "Pardon me, sir. Are you talking to me?"

I realize I had spoken the words aloud and say, "It's something I'm writing, C-3PO. While we wait for Star Wars Celebration to start."

You meet all kinds in line for these Star Wars conventions. So, it's no big deal when you find yourself sitting next to C-3PO—or a cosplayer indistinguishable from him.

This "C-3PO" flips up the front of his mask revealing the kindly face of a man in his autumn years. He extends his metal-gloved hand.

"A pleasure to meet you," he says around a charming smile. "I am Anthony. The little fellow inside the R2-unit beside me is Kenny."

To Anthony's right is a perfect replica of R2-D2. The droid's dome cracks open an inch or two, and from inside there's a flash of bright eyes and wriggling fingers waving hello. Then the dome clicks shut, and a fusillade of *beeps* and *boops* erupt from the costumed robot as it jostles cheerfully back and forth.

"He would like to know what you're writing. He seems to think it's about him."

"You understand those noises?" I ask incredulously. "The beeps make no sense to me."

Anthony pulls down his mask, and once again I'm staring into C-3PO's illuminated eyes.

"I *am* fluent in over six million forms of communication," Anthony quips in a perfect imitation of the movie character. "What is it you're writing, sir?" He gestures to the computer in my lap and the words I had just typed.

"Oh, it's a book about R2 and Zen."

C-3PO/Anthony straightens up in surprise.

"The stormtrooper turned Resistance fighter?"

"Not 'Finn,' *Zen*. It's a way of living that unlocks profound happiness and wisdom. It's the path of insight and compassion that brings freedom and unsurpassed appreciation for life."

"That is a great many things for such a small word," the C-3PO lookalike replies. "I don't see what R2 has to do with any of them. Are you sure you're not thinking of Master Yoda?"

Despite what my new friend thinks, there is a lot R2 *can* teach us about Zen.

"Just give me some time and I'll explain," I say out loud.

"Oh, we have plenty of that, sir," C-3PO/Anthony says, placing a hand on R2's head. "Ever since BB-8 came around, there's not a lot for R2 and I to do."

EPISODE II

R2 SAVES THE DAY

"Okay, C-3PO—err, I mean Anthony, we've got several hours until the opening ceremonies of Star Wars Celebration. Where should we start?"

"Please allow me the pleasure of this conceit, sir. When my mask is on call me 3PO."

"Gladly," I say. "And I'll call Kenny, R2. Sound good?"

"Excellent choice, sir. To answer your question about where to start, I typically prefer the beginning," 3PO says. He tilts his head to listen as Kenny makes a series of beeps from inside R2. "R2 agrees. The beginning is the best place to start."

"In that case, let's begin with Bodhidharma."

"Very good, sir. R2 and I visited there once. Humid planet. Very hard on the joints."

"Bodhidharma isn't a planet, 3PO. He's a man. A monk. From Earth. A sage who is credited with founding Zen Buddhism."

Bodhidharma (pronounced *bo-dee-dar-ma*) was a Buddhist monk living sometime in the fifth century. He traveled from India (or Afghanistan) to China to share Buddhism with the people of that region. When he got there, he was not pleased with what he found.

China at the time was a hotbed of philosophical discourse and emerging ideas. People were eager to learn new ways of thinking and use that knowledge to create a better life. Buddhist writings had recently been translated into the local language, and the Chinese took to them with vigor, debating the merits of Buddhism alongside homegrown philosophies like Confucianism and Taoism.

Unfortunately, much of Buddhism in China became steeped in superstition. People believed it could grant magical power or provide riches in the next life. Many rulers built Buddhist temples and dagobas—these were tombs housing Buddhist relics, not swampy planets hiding fugitive Jedi masters—to gain merit that would benefit them above others. Intellectuals spent much of their time systematizing Buddhist concepts and debating the finer philosophical points of the Buddha's teachings instead of living life the way he modeled and advised.

Bodhidharma came upon all this and became very grumpy.

"You can see for yourself just how grumpy. Look at these pictures," I say, calling up Bodhidharma's image on my browser.

R2 emits a high-pitched squeal. From inside, Kenny makes his domed head spin around like a top.

"I heartily agree with R2, sir," 3PO says. "What a terrifying visage. Rather reminiscent of Master Luke on Ahch-To, I'm afraid."

"There are similarities between those two masters, 3PO," I reply.

Luke had grown disenchanted with the Jedi Order and it's no wonder Bodhidharma wasn't happy with the version of Buddhism he discovered in China. To say it had wandered a bit off the path would perhaps be an understatement. The written teachings that the intellectuals were fussing over conveyed much of Buddhism's deepest insight, but the Chinese had turned that wisdom into mental games and word play. Chinese Buddhists sat around smugly and argued in clever little debates about the nature of reality, the meaning of life, and the definition of wisdom.

The intellectuals had lost the essence of the Buddha's teachings and turned it into mere philosophy concerned with fancy concepts and ideas, and sounding smart.

R2 beeps and whistles.

"R2 says they sound like a hive of mindless philosophers," translates C-3PO.

I nod. "Philosophies that don't help us improve how we live are a waste of time."

And Bodhidharma set out to show the early Buddhists of China just how much time they'd wasted. He left their ivory towers, echoing with their babbling voices, and entered a mountain cave in silence. For the next nine years, he stayed in that cave saying nothing and practicing meditation almost exclusively.

"In fact, that's how Zen got its name. Zen means meditation. And *zazen*—the practice modern Zen Buddhists do every day—literally translates as 'sitting meditation.'"

Meditation was Bodhidharma's response to the excessive talk and conceptual gobbledygook of his contemporaries. It was as though he was telling them, *You talk and debate and intellectualize—but the true meaning of Buddhism is not found in your words or ideas. It is found in the silence one experiences when the thinking and talking have stopped. It's a direct pointing at the heart of reality.*

Legend has it that Bodhidharma was so committed to making this point as clear as possible that he ripped off his eyelids—that way he wouldn't fall asleep and would be able to give more time to meditation.

"How ghastly," chimes C-3PO. "But I do not see what this Bodhidharma person has to do with R2."

"Look at R2's radar eye," I say. "Do you see an eyelid?"

C-3PO's head pivots from me to R2 and back to me as if he can't believe what I'm suggesting.

"But, sir! You can't possibly believe—"

"And then there's Bodhidharma's commitment to meditation," I continue, ignoring 3PO's protest. "If I recall correctly, R2 spent several years in meditative silence after Kylo Ren burned down Luke's Jedi Temple."

"I would not call low-power mode meditative silence—"

"But most of all, it's Bodhidharma's emphasis on direct experience and wholehearted action, rather than thinking and debating about abstract ideas, that most reminds me of R2-D2. You see, 3PO, Zen is the art of directly experiencing life as it is. It's about living wholeheartedly in the present moment."

Living wholeheartedly in the present means being fully attentive to the here and now. For example, you brush your teeth wholeheartedly when your mind is actively brushing them along with your toothbrush, hand, and mouth. When your mind is daydreaming or making plans, you can't experience tooth-brushing directly, and because life is only lived in the present, that means you missed out on part of it. If your mind is always in the clouds, you miss out on all of it. So, the first step of Zen is to be here now.

"Sound familiar, R2?"

C-3PO translates the little droid's beeps and boops, "My counterpart says he remembers being cold and wet when he heard something like that—from Master Yoda."

"That's right. R2 was outside Yoda's hut on Dagobah when the Jedi master was scolding Luke for daydreaming and never paying attention.

"This one a long time have I watched," Yoda said of Luke. "All his life how he looked away . . . to the future, the horizon. Never his mind on where he was. Hmm? What he was doing. Hmph."

Paying attention and wholeheartedly acting in the present is how we come to fully appreciate life, understand its mysteries, and know the right thing to do in each moment. And it is the only way to be fully alive.

R2 embodies the spirit of direct experience and wholehearted action without even trying (which is the only way do it, really). R2 behaves intuitively. He acts spontaneously.

When something needs to be done, R2 does it—without hesitation and with no thought of self-interest, results, or reward. Such wholehearted and direct action is one of the hallmarks of living the way Zen teaches.

"See, 3PO, a person who practices Zen responds constructively to what's needed in the present. You can't do that if you're daydreaming or if your head is filled with a bunch of concepts and ideas, like those ancient Chinese philosophers. Ideas don't save the day. Action does. And no one saves the day with direct action quite like R2-D2.

"Let's see how . . ."

EPISODE II

R2 DOESN'T HAVE DELUSIONS OF GRANDEUR

Remember the time Leia and company were fleeing Cloud City in the *Millennium Falcon*? Imperial agents were hot on their trail, but Lando and Chewbacca had the ship primed to finally throw off Darth Vader's pursuit.

"All right, Chewie. Ready for lightspeed," Lando said from the pilot's seat.

"If your people fixed the hyperdrive," Leia pointed out. "All the coordinates are set. It's now or never."

"Punch it!" cried Lando.

The coordinates may have been ready, but the hyperdrive wasn't. The engine coughed and spluttered like one of General Grevious' wheezing fits, and instead of rocketing to lightspeed, the *Falcon* just limped through space on sublight engines, leaving Leia, Chewie, Lando, and Luke vulnerable to Vader and his star destroyer's grasping tractor beam.

There was no hope of escape this time.

At least that's how things appeared. But even when things seem to be at their worst, they may be the very conditions needed for everything to go right. You just have to look at things from the right point of view.

Bodhidharma went into his cave to teach the Chinese the importance of meditation. He showed them that the better life they sought could only be found in direct experience. When you meditate the way Bodhidharma taught, you directly experience your mind, you "look deeply" into it. When you examine your mind, you come to understand how your thinking and perceptions create your view of the world, including your ideas of happiness, success, and tragedy—like the pending disaster the *Falcon* crew was facing. Looking deeply doesn't require thinking. It's more like actively observing, and it's what happens when you wholeheartedly engage the present. Through direct experience you recognize that your worst nightmares "depend largely on your own point of view," to paraphrase Obi-Wan Kenobi. Your point of view is colored by conditioning, judgment, personal experience, even whether you are tired or hungry. But when you aren't caught by one point of view or another, and you are open to possibilities, what seems like disaster may really be your salvation.

Let's return to the *Falcon*.

In the back of the ship, R2 was repairing C-3PO.

"Why don't we just go into lightspeed?" C-3PO wondered aloud.

R2 beeped in response.

"We can't? How would you know the hyperdrive is deactivated?" C-3PO demanded. "The city's central computer told you? R2-D2, you know better than to trust a strange computer."

R2 didn't like being lectured by his ungrateful patient. He burned C-3PO with his arc welder.

"Ouch! Pay attention to what you're doing!"

But R2 was paying attention to what he was doing. He was responding to the most immediate need—the hyperdrive.

While Lando panicked and Leia stressed and Chewie growled, R2 rolled to the rescue.

"R2, come back at once!" 3PO ordered. "You haven't finished with me yet! You don't know how to fix the hyperdrive. Chewbacca can do it. I'm standing here in pieces, and you're having delusions of grandeur!"

The only person deluded was C-3PO. R2 saw things with perfect clarity.

That's what people who embody Zen do. They see clearly and then they act appropriately. They aren't fooled by perceptions of fairness or who is at fault (like Lando). They aren't fixated on their small, self-centered needs (like C-3PO). They aren't flustered by overthinking repair strategies (like Chewbacca). Because they live lives of direct experience, their minds aren't cluttered with useless concepts. They simply see what needs to be done and they do it.

He certainly did, didn't he, 3PO?

In the convention center waiting room, 3PO hesitates. I can almost see the gears working inside his head. Finally he admits, "R2 has been known to get things right . . . from time to time. Had it not been for the city central computer, however, I doubt very much he would have ever known the *Millennium Falcon*'s hyperdrive was deactivated and not damaged. There would have been no heroics in that case."

It may seem pure happenstance that the Cloud City computer gave R2 that vital piece of information about the *Falcon*'s lightspeed engine. Han Solo might even call it luck. But stuff like that just seems to happen to people who live lives of direct experience. Less attached to a point of view or conventional thinking, they discover wisdom in the most unlikely places, create amazing works of art out of common garbage, dispel a wounded heart with a well-timed word . . . or notice important data about deactivated engines while unlocking a docking bay door.

When your head isn't filled with the usual noise, you've got plenty of space for the unexpected to come your way—and you can recognize its value when it does. "You're quite correct, sir," C-3PO says. "R2's head is rather empty."

"Ah, good one, 3PO." I grin. "But Zen doesn't look so unfavorably on empty heads."

Remember, Bodhidharma rejected the overly philosophical ways of the early Chinese Buddhists. All their intellectual pursuits had tangled their minds with a jumble of half-understood concepts that were meant to help them understand the world but, because they were overly enamored with the ideas, only made everything more confusing. To gain clarity, they needed to empty their minds of all their pedantic expertise and return to the state of a beginner. As Yoda would say, they needed to *unlearn what they had learned*.

"Unlearn what they had learned?" C-3PO questions.

"That's right," I say. "Yoda's expression is very Zen-like, and it connects nicely to the idea of beginner's mind."

It was Bodhidharma's belief that the "empty" mind of a beginner would realize the truth the Buddha was pointing out more easily than the cluttered mind of the expert. So, he taught the Chinese philosophers by example. Through meditation they would unlearn all the useless concepts they had learned.

One modern Zen teacher named Shunryu Suzuki summed it up like this: "If your mind is empty, it is always ready for anything; it is open to everything. In the beginner's mind there are many possibilities, but in the expert's there are few."

"Remind me again how many languages you speak, 3PO," I ask.

"I am fluent in over six million forms of communication."

"That's amazing! I can barely speak one. It would seem you're quite the expert, then. And yet you're rather deaf to the emotional subtleties of human communication, something a droid like R2, with minimal language skills, understands fluently."

"I don't know what you mean."

"Exactly. I'm thinking of the time you broke up that 'closed-door committee meeting' between Han and Leia on the *Millennium Falcon* to report that you isolated the ship's reverse power flux coupling (that was their first kiss, you know). Or the time you interrupted their reunion outside Maz Kanata's ruined castle to show off your new red arm."

C-3PO seems to frown. "Oh, dear. That was a most loathsome appendage."

R2 might not be an expert communicator, but he does know how to read the room, as it were, and respond accordingly. That's the benefit of a mind that's "always ready for anything and open to everything." It doesn't have all the answers, but it's attentive enough to the world to allow the appropriate response to arise naturally. Just like R2 always does.

Time after time we see R2 flying into action when words would only muddle the situation. Other times he's there with an empathetic whistle or inspiring boop to give Luke or Anakin the encouragement they need.

R2 just seems to know the right thing to do or the right thing to say.

And then there was that one time he said nothing and let someone else do the talking for him. . . .

EPISODE IV

R2 PULLS A
CHEAP MOVE

"No, you most definitely *do not*, R2-D2!" C-3PO replies
to something R2 said while I was at the concession stand. "I
don't care what this strange man says. My facilities are tai-
lored to the highest standards of human communication!"

"What's all this about?" I ask, retaking my place in line.

C-3PO, who is clearly flustered, replies, "Now R2
thinks he knows more than I—a protocol droid—about
communication."

"Well . . . he does seem to get through to people pretty
easily, 3PO."

"But I am programmed for etiquette and protocol!"

"Doing what's best sometimes means ignoring etiquette
and protocol," I say. "The unconventional approach can

often be the solution to thorny problems. That's what R2 has taught us."

"He has?"

"Of course!"

Let me set the scene.

Luke Skywalker had just learned his old friend, Han Solo, is dead. They had not seen each other for years. Not since Luke had cut himself off from the Force after failing to train Han's son, Ben, to be a Jedi.

Now a new student named Rey is at Luke's doorstep, seeking training and his help in the struggle against the dark side. But Luke is no longer the hero Rey had heard about from tales of the Galactic Civil War. Luke has lost his faith in the Jedi Order. He now believes the path of the Jedi is the way of failure—it only creates pain and destruction.

Luke refuses to train Rey. He refuses to repeat the mistakes of the past. After all, it was his fault Han died, he believes. By failing Ben, he had set the son on course to killing his father.

Luke rebuffs Rey and, in a conflicted state, he enters the *Millennium Falcon* in the dead of night. Maybe he sought solace in the memories stowed aboard that junky freighter. Maybe he hoped to find forgiveness from the ghost of the captain he so utterly let down.

The only thing we know for certain was that Luke believed it was *"time for the Jedi to end."* The galaxy would be better off if the light of the Jedi was extinguished forever. That way no more students would fall to the dark side. No more fathers would have to die.

Luke seated himself beside the ship's dejarik table and hung his head. In a nearby corner, resting silently like Bodhidharma in his cave, was the very same little astromech that gamed Chewbacca over that circular table many years before.

The droid shifted, drawing Luke's attention.

Luke looked up. "R2!"

The eyes of the despondent Jedi master shone brightly at that moment for the first time in ages. His loyal companion had come back to him. Through Luke's grizzly beard and careworn face, the young farm boy from Tatooine is evident once again.

R2 greeted Luke in his usual colorful manner.

"Hey, sacred island. Watch the language," Luke said. Then in response to something R2 presumably said about Luke returning to help his friends fight evil, Luke refused again, saying, "Old friend. I wish I could make you understand. But I'm not coming back. Nothing can make me change my mind."

Luke would never leave his island again.

Someone else might feel defeated or even angered by Luke's response. But R2 had beginner's mind—he was attentive to what Luke said and, more importantly (and unconventionally), what he didn't say.

"What he *didn't* say?" demands 3PO. "How quaint!"

I shrug. "Sometimes what people don't say reveals more about their mind than what they actually express."

R2 heard the unspoken subtext beneath Luke's refusal to leave the sacred island: the despair, the regret, and the fear. He could hear what wasn't said because the beginner's mind *listens*—and it is open to possibilities. The expert mind is closed. It doesn't listen; it preaches. It wants the other person to hurry up and finish what they're saying, so it can jump in and give its expert advice. It believes it has all the answers.

In the final years of the Republic, many Jedi had lost their beginner's mind. In their arrogance, they thought they were the final word on all matters of knowledge and the sole proprietors of truth. One senior Jedi, Jocasta Nu, said in reference to the Jedi's vast warehouse of knowledge, *"If an item does not appear in our records, it does not exist."*

The expert mind isn't just closed to possibilities, it would seem, but to reality itself. Nu denied the existence of an entire planet because the "infallible" Jedi archives came up empty when Obi-Wan searched for information on the cloning world of Kamino.

As it was with Nu, the expert mind had blinded the Jedi to the actual circumstances of the real world. They denied the re-emergence of the Sith, the erosion of their ideals, and the corruption of their beloved Republic. They were the experts, after all. How could they be wrong?

Long after the fall of the Republic, Luke told R2 straight out that there was nothing he could say that would get him to leave his island and train another generation in the failed ways of the Jedi. The expert mind would hear that and take it as a challenge. It would argue. It would reason. It would bully with its superior logic and "facts." In the end, it would only force Luke to become more entrenched in his stance because he would have never felt heard, never felt understood.

But R2 listened and understood what Luke had left unsaid.

It takes compassion to listen to another person in pain—to sit in silence with an open mind and refrain from trying to fix their problems. Compassion is born from the beginner's mind, the open mind that accepts the person for who they are in this moment right now. Listening compassionately is how you understand the other person's feelings and their point of view. Then you will know how best to respond—or not respond!—and be able to meet them where they are.

Luke wasn't refusing to leave his island because he had become callous to the needs of others. He was refusing because he deeply cared about them. Compassion was alive in him as much as it was in R2. Luke didn't want the weaknesses of the Jedi to bring any more harm to the galaxy.

"A Jedi was responsible for the rise of Darth Vader," Luke told Rey, denigrating the Jedi for their failures like only an "expert" could.

"Yes! And another Jedi for saving him," she replied with the simple truth obvious to beginners.

The Jedi that "saved" Vader, of course, was Luke himself. It was Luke's compassion for his father that helped Vader find redemption and bring an end to evil in the galaxy. (At least for a while.)

R2 recognized that Luke was torn. His compassion to help others was the reason why he refused to leave the island. But withdrawing from the fight and allowing the Jedi to die out was not the kind of help people were looking for. They needed Luke Skywalker, rebel leader, Jedi Master. They needed the hero who left Tatooine to rescue a princess and found himself saving the galaxy. When you listen with compassion and the mind of a beginner, you see possibilities you'd otherwise miss.

Luke said he would not leave the island and nothing would change his mind.

But R2's beginner's mind—open to all possibilities—saw an opportunity the conventional mind might have missed.

So, R2 let Leia do the talking for him.

General Kenobi, years ago you served my father in the Clone Wars . . .

Leia's message, pulled up from R2's inexhaustible memory bank, came to life, projecting the same holographic image of the princess that first called Luke into service over thirty years before. The compassion he had to help people fight the Empire back then, R2 thought, would remind him of his duty to aid those in need now.

On the sacred island, Luke watched the holographic recording of his sister, heard her plea—*"Help me, Obi-Wan Kenobi. You're my only hope"*—and knew this time it was meant for him. He had taken on the role of self-exiled–Jedi-master-called-back-to-service once played by Obi-Wan.

This time Luke was the galaxy's only hope.

At that time, Luke crimped his eyes at R2 and grumbled, *"That was a cheap move!"*

It wasn't so much cheap as it was insightful and effective. That's the benefit of listening with the beginner's mind.

"Excuse me, sir," C-3PO says after R2 emits a series of beeps. "R2 suggests this beginner's mind is not unlike a Jedi power. He reminded me of a time on Tatooine when Master Kenobi used the Force to fool Imperial Stormtroopers searching for us."

"No, 3PO. Beginner's mind isn't at all like the Jedi Mind Trick."

Beginner's mind isn't a power or even a skill we develop, like cooking or rancor-taming. It's more of an attitude, a way to live life fully and effortlessly. It is the mind's natural state before thinking, comparing, and judging scrabble things up.

The first time you do something new you have a natural attitude of what we have been calling direct experience or wholehearted action. You are alert, curious, attentive. You do the thing—say tying your custom Vans x Star Wars shoes—with your full presence. Tying shoes is interesting and exciting when it's new, and you have no trouble giving it your undivided attention—the first hundred times or so. After a while, however, shoe-tying becomes easier and you lose your beginner's attitude. Your mind drifts away from the shoelaces as you tie them. You forget the difficulty you had the first time you looped the laces into bunny ears. Eventually you tie your Yoda-print shoes and don't even realize you did it until after the fact. You've become an expert, and you no longer have the time to pay attention to something so mundane as shoe-tying.

Let's hear from Suzuki again: "In the beginner's mind there is no thought, 'I have attained something.'" (Not even mastery of lacing Star Wars sneakers, I'm sure he would agree.) "All self-centered thoughts limit our vast mind. When we have no thought of achievement, no thought of self, we are true beginners. Then we can really learn something."

R2 is not concerned about personal achievement. He has no self-centered thoughts. He bravely faced Imperials, Jawas, even Tusken Raiders in the Jundland Wastes to fulfill his mission and deliver Leia's message to Obi-Wan Kenobi. When he delivered that message in full for the first time in Obi-Wan's hut, he saw the effect it had on Luke, how it called him to adventure and inspired him to serve and to be part of something bigger then himself.

The attentive mind of a true beginner takes note of things like this. With no thought of personal achievement, it's able to "really learn something" about the people and world around it.

You might remember Luke refused the call to adventure in Obi-Wan's hut just like he did on the sacred island.

"I can't get involved!" he said. *"I've got work to do! It's not that I like the Empire. I hate it. But there's nothing I can do about it right now. It's such a long way from here."*

Sounds reminiscent of his there's-nothing-you-can-say-that-will-change-my-mind routine on the sacred island. Doesn't it?

I guess old Luke's character isn't all that drastically different from the younger version.

But, despite the thirty-plus-year history between playing Leia's recording, R2 does not let his experience with Luke stop him from seeing his friend again for the first time. That's the beginner's attitude: to face each thing like it's your first time. You may have tied your shoes 9,999 times, but the beginner's mind meets the 10,000th time as it truly is—the first.

C-3PO lifts his hand and says, "The first? Whatever do you mean?"

"I mean each moment is unique and one of a kind. Each moment is a first."

You are not the same person now as you were back when you learned to tie your shoes. The size of your fingers, the laces, your state of mind—all different. Each time you tie your shoes, take a step in them, scrape gum off the sole is a first, even if you've done it a thousand times. No moment is exactly like another. Isn't that reason enough to cherish them?

The present moment may echo the past, but it's always original.

When R2 saw Luke on the sacred island, he met him again for the first time. He met Luke with the empty mind of a beginner just like he did back on Tatooine, when Luke felt compassion to help people but was hesitant to get involved. R2 saw through grizzly Luke's grumpiness on the island and recognized the same conflicted boy from back in the day. The boy from the past echoed in the man of the present. The natural response for R2 was to replay Leia's message.

That recording may not have spurred Luke into action immediately (it took a bit more coaxing—both on Tatooine long ago and the sacred island), but it did encourage him to share his concerns with Rey, to open up to her about why he had sequestered himself and why the Jedi way should end. And it convinced him to teach her about the true nature of the Force.

R2 offers some beeps and whistles.

"My friend asks if Bodhidharma taught the ways of the Force," 3PO says.

"Not exactly. But before we get to that, we need to talk about R2's nature. Just what exactly does Zen have to say about the true essence of that kind-yet-sometimes-nasty little astromech?"

Turn the page and find out.

EPISODE V

R2 TAKES A
PERSONALITY QUIZ

"Hey, 3PO. Did you hear this one: What does the Force do each morning?"

"Sir . . . ?

"The Force awakens, grabs a cup of coffee, and rushes out the door for work."

"My interpretation protocol must be malfunctioning. R2, do you know what he's talking about?"

"It's a joke, 3PO. Remember the movie title . . . *The Force A w a k e n s . . .*? Never mind."

"Ah . . . yes, of course. Most amusing!" C-3PO stammers before bending over and whispering, "R2, sometimes I just don't understand human behavior."

In *The Force Awakens,* something inside Rey that has *"always been there"* awakens. She inexplicably finds herself using the Force to pilot the *Millennium Falcon* through miraculous maneuvers, mind-trick a stormtrooper into releasing her from imprisonment, and out-lightsaber the seasoned dark-sider Kylo Ren. Her awakening throws open of the floodgate of her innate potential.

According to Zen, you have a similar potential inside you that has also "always been there." Like Rey, you can wake up to this potential, though calling it "potential" isn't quite right because it is not something you *develop* or *become*—it is who you truly are without trying to be something different. It is who you are right now and have always been. This something is your true nature, what Zen teachers call *buddha nature.*

"Buddha? I am familiar with this word," 3PO interjects knowingly. "It applies to the fat golden statue some of the people of your planet worship as a god. As I am both golden and worshiped as a god, I can of course relate to this. Although my worshipers are much furrier and more adorable than the ones in this system. And of course I am far slimmer than Master Buddha, too."

"You are rather svelt, 3PO. But the fat golden guy you refer to isn't the Buddha. That's Budai or Hotei, a jolly monk who has come to represent a welcoming and open sentiment. That's why you find 'the laughing monk' near the door of a lot of Chinese restaurants.

"The historic Buddha, on the other hand, was almost as thin as you. And his name wasn't actually Buddha. 'Buddha' is a sort of title that means 'the awakened one.'

It was given to the founder of Buddhism, a man named Siddhartha Gautama. He wasn't fat like I said, and he certainly wasn't golden or a god and no right-minded person worships him. Siddhartha was the first person to wake up to a simple truth that freed him from a lot of searching and suffering. When he shared this insight with the world, people called him Buddha. The root of the word *buddha* is the same as *bodhi*, as in *Bodhi*dharma. Both basically mean 'awakening.' When you wake up, you're no longer caught in a dream or an idea of reality, but engaging with it directly as it is, without the usual mental clutter and confusion."

R2 chirps and 3PO translates, "There goes Bodhi now."

I look up as a guy dressed in Imperial fatigues walks by on his way to the bathroom. He has signature goggles strapped to the top of his head that indicate he is dressed as Bodhi, the Imperial defector who helped steal the plans to the original Death Star.

"Bodhi had an awakening too, of sorts," I say. "Leaving the Empire as he did, but whether his defection was the result of a Zen-like awakening to his true nature or the realization he was serving an evil regime is, I suppose, open to debate."

All of Zen is directing us to awaken to our true nature, to dispel the illusion of concepts, of knowing, of separate self. When Bodhidharma entered his cave to meditate, he didn't need to say a single word. His action said all that needed saying. And what it said reverberated across all of China—even down to us here and now.

Sit. Be still. See your true nature.

That is the purpose of meditation: to see your true self, to wake up to the boundless reality of buddha nature, of who you truly are.

"Sir, I don't need meditation to know who I am. I am a service droid. Programmed for etiquette and protocol."

"That's your job, 3PO. But who are you *really*?"

Who am I? It's a question people have been asking since the beginning of time. It's a question many of us have asked since we first formed the belief that we are individuals separate from the world around us. You may not even realize you've been asking that question, but it's always there in the background like a busy analysis droid researching and cataloging your experiences in the hope of defining the world and your place in it.

Who am I?

It starts when you're quite young. People ask, "What's your favorite color? What do you want to be when you grow up? What's your favorite food?"

When we're kids, we delight in answering these questions because it gives us a sense of power over a world beyond our immediate control. Power to a kid is especially attractive because we have so little influence over our own lives when we're young. From the moment we wake, we are told what to do and what not to do. Our every waking moment is regimented and monitored by well-meaning parents who try to impart the rules of living a good life and the behavioral expectations of society. But to children, it's like living under constant Imperial rule—freedoms are denied for the professed sake of safety and order, and any resistance is met with swift and irresistible discipline.

It's no wonder we become enamored with figures of great power like Jedi and Sith (and the various superheroes also owned by our supreme entertainment overlord, the Disney Company. All hail our glorious masters!—and all rights reserved.).

But when we, as kids, are asked what we prefer—pizza or burritos, blue or red—we are finally granted the opportunity to exert a little authority of our own. It's not much, but it is something, and it stirs the lust for more.

With each passing year that authority expands and the desire to define ourselves by our preferences becomes more and more pronounced. We get good grades in math or have a proclivity for art, and we latch on to these things as defining attributes of our character. We take online personality quizzes and develop a sense of who we are based on their results ("What Star Wars Movie Are You?" "Which Wizarding House Do You Belong To?" "Are You an Introvert, an Extrovert, or an Ambivert?"). We build our self-image based on the sports teams we like, the music we listen to, the clothing brands we prefer. We may even use labels related to pastimes: cosplayer or sports fan, athletic or bookish, Jedi Padawan or Sith apprentice.

When we're older, who we are is defined by our chosen career path. We introduce ourselves by saying, "I am a: (doctor, a bus-driver, a teacher, a monk, an engineer, a ventriloquist.)"

We also define ourselves by our nationality and family heritage. "I am Italian; George Lucas is my seventh cousin twice removed; my great, great, great grandfather was the earl of Fort Lauderdale."

This quest for self-identity was particularly pronounced in Rey. In her case, the resolution of her ancestry—specifically who her parents were—was like a Star Wars Holy Grail for her as well as for an audience that had become intrigued with the mystery of who this girl was and why she exhibited such incredible strength in the Force. The question "Who am I?" drove Rey into the dark side grotto beneath the surface of Luke's sacred island on the planet Ahch-To.

She found herself in that cave—countless versions of herself standing in a line that stretched beyond sight—and voiced aloud, *"Show me my parents."* Rey wanted to know where she came from, who she was.

R2 whirs and beeps, and C-3PO translates.

"My counterpart is curious about Rey's rather peculiar experience. What does it mean?"

"We'll discuss that more later, 3PO. For now, what's important is understanding Rey's desire to define her identity, to know her roots, her background."

I mentioned before that our journey toward self-discovery begins when we are quite young, after we first formed the belief that we are individuals separate from the people around us. This belief leaves us feeling isolated and detached from the world we inhabit. When we discovered "me" and realized that "I exist," we lost that sense of shared existence we had with our parents, our playthings, our pets and siblings. In Star Wars terms, we lost our connection to the Force, to the connection we share with "all living things," as Obi-Wan might say.

We find that, although we share a home with others, we are alone. Our parents can't read our thoughts and they can't see us when the door is shut.

We are on our own, seemingly isolated in a cold uncaring universe.

That is why we exert so much energy defining our identity—to stake out something solid in a world that seems so unstable. With a defined identity, we can find like-minded people or ideologies that give us at least a semblance of that state of belonging, that sense of being home, we lost as children.

"I felt alone when my maker left me to become a Jedi," says 3PO in a melancholy tone. "But I found my place serving his mother and then Mistress Padmé before I came into Princess Leia's service."

R2 chirps instructively.

"That's right, R2. *General* Leia," responds 3PO. "Of course, I've never been alone since I met this greasy lunkhead." He gestures to the astromech at his side and adds in an undertone, "Even if I'd love a moment or two of solitude from time to time."

"That's a nice sentiment," I say. "But Zen says we are never really alone, that the place of belonging we seek is always present. We don't need to go anywhere or become anything to return home. Our true home is right here, right now."

In *The Force Awakens*, Maz Kanata saw that Rey was struggling to find her place in the galaxy. She took Rey's hand and told her, *"The belonging you seek is not behind you. It is ahead."*

Maz was trying to convince Rey that she could never go home again. The sense of belonging she lost when her parents abandoned her could never be reclaimed. Home is in the future she builds, the path she blazes.

In a way Maz is right. Life is constant change. We can never return to the life we once had because it is only a memory that exists in the past. We may look back on it fondly, but it is no more real than a pleasant dream.

On the other hand, Maz's advice—wise as it may seem—isn't quite right because true belonging isn't something you achieve. You don't adopt an exotic ideology, join a new cause, or build a new house to find your true home. You don't become complete by attaining some self-prescribed goal that signifies you've finally "made it." You don't get your happily ever after when you join the "it" crowd or are inducted into the Jedi Council (that's right, I'm talking to you, Anakin!).

Try any of it or all of it and you'll see. The luster of every win fades when the newness wears off.

No victory lasts forever, and you can never find your true home outside yourself.

You find it by meeting yourself where you are right now.

And right now.

And right now.

When you are stable, and your mind is clear, you will see that everything you really need you already have. At this moment, you are already whole because you've been home where you belong all along.

"Ugh, I'd fancy being home right now. In my bed," Anthony grouses, lifting the front of his mask and breaking the illusion of C-3PO. "Sitting on the floor for so long is giving me bedsores." He tilts his head to listen to R2's groans. "Kenny concurs. When will they let us in and start the bloody opening ceremonies?"

Let me be clear by what I mean by home. Home is when you are at ease in your existence, when you are at peace in the present and know that you belong—regardless of the structure over your head, the labels you use to define yourself, or the hardness of the concrete floor inside a 10,000-person waiting room.

And before you start to grumble about the cheery vapidity of "home" like a callous Han Solo dismissing hokey religions, let me say home is not some naïve state of mind where you think everything is sunshine and gimer sticks. Being home doesn't mean you think everything is perfect. It means you're not struggling to make it perfect, that you see the beauty in the imperfection and understand that "perfection" is just a concept people use to drive themselves crazy.

Home means not laboring to become anyone or anything, not struggling to make the world conform to your choosing or make yourself fit the way you think the world wants you to be. It's being at ease with your existence—like R2.

"He *is* rather sure of himself," Anthony says in his C-3PO voice, his mask once again covering his face.

You can always improve. The world can always get better. But that improvement comes a lot more swiftly and sticks around a lot longer when you aren't hung up on the concept of improvement.

You remodel your home from a place of stability and freedom. That's what being "home" means. It's being free where you are right now.

Rey searched for a place of belonging never realizing she was arriving at her true home with every step she took.

"R2 says he knows what you mean, but I'm afraid this is all quite beyond my capacity," 3PO says.

"Buddhism says understanding is available to everyone. Even mindless philosophers like you and me, 3PO."

"As you say, sir. However, I do have my doubts."

"Don't worry, 3PO."

It'll all become clearer in the next chapter.

DOES A DROID HAVE BUDDHA NATURE?

Let's return to Luke's sacred island.

It's the morning after R2 convinced Luke to teach Rey about the Force. Although Luke agreed to instruct her with the sole purpose of showing her why the Jedi Order should come to an end, his teachings are no less meaningful.

He guided Rey to a rock on a cliff and ordered her to *"sit–legs crossed."* There's a brief gag with a leaf and an outstretched hand trying to physically touch the Force, and then Luke got down to business.

He took Rey's hand and lowered it, so her fingers were pressed firmly against the rock—literally and figuratively grounding her to reality.

"Breathe," he told Rey, giving her one of the most funda-
mental Zen instructions. "Just breathe. Reach out with your
feelings."

Zen invites people to "just breathe" to help them turn
off intentional thinking and pay attention to their body
and how it naturally inhales and exhales. The mind stays
present with the breath as it comes and goes. This is how
we begin to unclutter our busy minds and see things with
greater clarity and develop more solidity, like a certain heroic astromech.

Similarly, Luke is encouraging Rey to slow down her
overactive mind, to ground herself in the present and "feel"
the world around her—to see it as it is before her mind
labels, measures, and discriminates.

Following Luke's instructions, Rey reached out, not with her
hand as before, but with her heart and mind.

"What do you see?" Luke asked.

Rey describes a vision of complementary opposites, balanced components of a complete whole. She sees Luke's
island home on the planet Ahch-To. She sees life blossom
and die. She sees warmth and cold, peace, and violence.
And between each of these harmonious pairs there is balance, energy, the Force.

"And inside you?" Luke probed, hoping to drive home
his lesson that the Force is bigger than himself, bigger than
the Jedi, even while it is as small as the breath of a young
woman meditating on a rock.

Rey smiled. "That same Force."

That Force is where Rey belongs. It is her true home and
it is always with her.

The Force is the connective tissue that bridges life and death, birth and decay, and connects Rey with all existence. It is the energy that binds the galaxy together.

"You must feel the Force around you," Yoda once told Luke, *"between you, the rock, the tree. Everywhere."*

If the Force is everywhere, how can Rey be separated from it? If it is inside Rey and outside of her, where does the Force begin and Rey end?

Is it even correct to ask about beginnings and endings?

When Luke was first introduced to the Force, Obi-Wan Kenobi told him, *"The Force is an energy field created by all living things. It surrounds us, penetrates us, binds the galaxy together."*

The Force is created by life. It surrounds everything. It penetrates everything. It is in Rey. It is outside Rey. That means it has no beginning. It has no end. In other words, the Force is everywhere, erasing the lines that separate Rey from the rock she touches and the rock that is touching her.

Certainly, Rey and the rock are not the same. We can distinguish Rey's hand from the rock she touches, and Rey can walk away from the rock, board the *Falcon*, and blast off from the planet, leaving the rock far behind.

But on a primordial level, the existence she shares with the rock can never be divided. The Force never leaves Rey. It will always connect her with the rock no matter how far she travels from it.

Through the Force, the distinction between Rey and the rock falls away. She is, *"from a certain point of view,"* interconnected with the Force and inseparable from everything in the galaxy.

This means the fulfillment Rey seeks in groups and family and father figures can be found in far more than the object of her desire. If she were to open up to the Force, she would see that this fulfillment is always available no matter where she finds herself. Being part of the Resistance may give her a profound sense of belonging (and there's nothing wrong with that), but that same sense of belonging is available wherever she finds herself in the galaxy—even Jakku.

Finding "home" wherever she is doesn't mean Rey would give up helping the Resistance. Quite the opposite. Her resolve to do good would be stronger and clearer by seeing how completely and indivisibly she is connected to the entire galaxy, not just a slice of it.

Compassion is the natural response of the awakened mind. Doing good automatically arises because you aren't caught by the distinction between "us and them."

Similarly, Zen teaches that the distinction we see between you and me, between the world and ourselves is merely a "point of view."

Reality is not made of separate energies like life and death, peace and violence at war with each other. The truth is these energies are in balance, a balance that makes up one big reality where all the little things we think exist separately actually exist in a mutual state of dependence.

This is a very profound perspective on the human condition, one that is hard to reconcile when we think in terms of good and evil, light and dark. And while it is true that these are different things, it is also true that you can't have one without the other. They coexist. They are part of our nondualistic reality.

The dark side and light side of the Force seem to suggest a clear and solid divide. But a more careful examination reveals that the Jedi agree with and profess the Zen insight of nondualism.

If we were to pull back from Rey and her rock and look at the floor of the chamber behind her, we would see a mosaic that looks like this drawing I just did:

R2 whistles plaintively.

3PO nods agreement. "It is rather an artless doodle, isn't it, R2."

"Well, it's not Sabine Wren, but I don't think it's that bad," I pout.

"What is it supposed to be, sir? A porg?"

"A p-porg?" I shout, exasperated. "It's the Prime Jedi!"

3PO eyes me warily and makes a show of covering his mouth with his hand. "I think this one could use more time in Bodhidharma's cave," he stage-whispers to R2.

The Prime Jedi, as the name suggests, was the first Jedi, the founder of the Jedi Order and perhaps the author of the original Jedi texts Rey steals out from under Luke's nose.

Seated in meditation, the Prime Jedi is central in the mosaic, balancing light on one side with darkness on the other.

"Equal number of Jedi and Sith," 3PO says. "Isn't that what is meant by the balance of the Force?"

"That might be taking things a bit too literally," I say.

On first blush, it may seem that the mosaic is suggesting a balance in quantity or equal parts darkness and equal parts light. This would be a dualistic view of reality, where light and dark are two distinct (and separate) energies struggling for dominance and have to be brought to heel and made to stay in their corner by a seasoned Jedi master.

But that interpretation doesn't jibe with what we know about the Force binding "everything" in the galaxy together. From Rey's vision on the rock to Obi-Wan's explanation on Tatooine to Yoda's teachings on Dagobah, we know that the Force connects things—it doesn't divide them.

When you look more closely at the mosaic, you see there is a circle of light in the dark and a circle of dark in the light. Within each is the seed of the other. This suggests something much different than a pair of dueling opposites. It suggests a state of inclusivity, where the light and dark aren't separate but part of a larger whole. What's more the circle enclosing the entire image is itself a symbol of totality, of wholeness. In other words, the mosaic is telling us it's all one big reality where all the little things we think exist separately actually exist in a mutual state of interdependence.

It's in this one big reality that we find ourselves. No matter where we are or when we are, we're always part of this shared existence. But instead of feeling at home where we are, we feel disconnected, isolated, lonely. We feel separate.

It starts when we conceive of ourselves as "I."

The question "who am I?" is based on the false premise that you have an inherent nature that is fixed and separate from the world around you. You try to discover that nature in your ancestry, your career, your preferences. You think if you peel back the layers of yourself like an onion, you will get to the core of who you really are—your true self. But when every layer is stripped away, you don't come to an inherent, fixed self—a soul that defines you. There is no seed at the center of the onion. Instead, you discover something quite extraordinary (and, at the same time, completely ordinary).

You discover the entire universe.

Luke learned early in his Jedi training that he could "feel the Force flowing through him." Rey expressed a similar insight: the Force is inside her. And Obi-Wan says it penetrates and binds the galaxy—that it connects everything. And as it connects, it "flows through" us.

Likewise, there is a "force" that connects you with everything. This force is, in fact, everything—it is the entire universe, including you, existing in a causal flow with everything else. You are not an inherent, fixed self that is separate from the universe around you. There is no "you" apart from the universe, and, conversely, no universe apart from you. You are an interdependent part of the world, changing from moment to moment as the world changes with you.

When you drop the concept of "you," you see how big, beautiful, and inclusive reality is. You recognize—much like Rey—the "balance" and "energy" that binds the universe together and how the fiction you created about your inherent, fixed self has distracted you from enjoying the world as it truly is. Without the concept of "you," you find you're already home where you belong; you wake up to the timelessness of reality and discover that it is pervaded by what Zen teachers call buddha nature.

Buddha nature is the profound peace, wisdom, and compassion that characterizes the entire universe.

You may think that when you clear away the static and get a clear picture of reality you'll find a cold, amoral, mechanistic universe. But according to witnesses since the time of the Buddha 2,600 years ago to the present day, that's not the case. The structure of the universe isn't sterile and heartless but is in fact characterized by buddha nature. It's moral, benevolent, compassionate, generous, and wise.

And because you have no inherent, fixed self separate from the universe that means buddha nature characterizes you too. The qualities of the Buddha and Bodhidharma— selflessness, stability, dignity, insight, spiritual freedom, and so forth—are equally yours. Of course, it's not quite right to say they are "yours" because there is no you to possess them, no you that develops freedom or becomes more stable or grows in generosity. Nonetheless, the wise, open, brilliant nature of the universe *is* your nature. It's only when you conceive of yourself as a fixed self separate from the universe that you lose touch with your true nature and become confused, frustrated, greedy, and desperate.

C-3PO lifts a golden hand. "Pardon me, sir. Are you suggesting that human nature is the same as this 'buddha nature'?"

"Basically, yeah."

"Remarkable. In my experience, there are few human beings I would call selfless, compassionate, or wise. Very few indeed."

"That's because the belief in the self is so deeply ingrained it muddles most of us up most of the time, and we become desperate to satisfy the fleeting preferences and needy demands of our clinging minds. But Bodhidharma showed by example that people can drop the fiction and put an end to their pointless efforts to satisfy their greedy, selfish habits. They just need to stop talking and thinking and start doing—like R2."

"But, sir! You've been talking about human beings. Does a droid have buddha nature?"

"That's a good question, 3PO, and we'll get to that. But first we need to talk a bit about nothing."

"Nothing? Whatever do you mean?"

"Let's turn the page and find out."

EPISODE VII

A PILOTED X-WING IS STILL EMPTY

"So, let's talk about nothing."

"How do you propose we do so, sir? As R2 points out, talking is expressly saying *something* and if nothing is said, one's actions cannot be described as *talking*."

"A lot can be communicated without speaking, 3PO. But never mind that for now. Tell me, what do you find when you peel away every layer of an onion?"

"According to your previous statement, sir, the entire universe. But in my personal experience preparing banquets for Senator Amidala, there is nothing left once all the layers of an onion are gone."

"Exactly. That's what I want to talk about."

"The entire universe or nothing?"

"What's the difference?"

When Buddhists talk about "nothing" they aren't being nihilistic. You'll never find a Buddhist monk moping around like a moody Kylo Ren brooding over the death mask of his evil grandfather.

"Nothing" to Buddhist ears doesn't have the same ring to it that it does to ours. "Nothing" is the last school bell before summer vacation starts. It is the concussive *boom* of the Death Star exploding, ending an era of tyranny. It is the exuberate exclamation that we are totally free.

"Nothing" is meant to convey the truth that can't be described using concepts or ideas because concepts and ideas aren't the way things actually are—they're just labels of them.

But "nothing" can be confusing, given the dreary, angsty, hopeless connotations associated with "nothing." That's why it's better to use a more accurate word to describe this joyful truth: "emptiness."

When we get to the center of an onion we find emptiness and, with it, the profound stillness of eternity.

"R2, if Aunt Beru showed you a cup brimming with blue milk and asked you if it was empty, what would you say?"

After a curt beep, 3PO speaks for the little astromech. "He says, 'No, it is not empty. It is filled with blue milk.'"

"If Aunt Beru pours the cup out on the parched Tatooine desert, what would you say then?"

C-3PO listens, then whacks R2 with his hand and exclaims, "'What a waste of blue milk!' R2, I don't think you're taking this seriously."

No, R2 wouldn't. Maybe that's why he's such a good model of Zen.

Most people would say the cup is empty. But, empty of what? Blue milk, certainly, but air? No, it's not empty of air. Maybe there's light photons in there and some sand particles too. Who knows?

This may all sound academic and a bit pointless, but it's important to understand that the word "empty" doesn't mean anything unless you know what something is empty of. To be empty is to be free of *something*.

When we peel back the layers of you, we discover that you are empty too—empty of a separate self. There is no soul, no fixed "you" that stands apart from the book you hold in your hands, the air in your lungs, or the personality you've inherited and honed over a lifetime. The "you" that sits there reading these lines is a product of the entire universe. No part distinct. No part separate. But together all the parts are a unique expression of everything that is.

According to Buddhism, you are an ever-changing flow of form, feelings, perceptions, thoughts, and consciousness—each, in turn, changing with the world around them. From moment to moment the world is a different place and you are a different person. When you peel back the layers of "you," you discover the limitless world.

Take R2 for instance.

"Uh, sir," 3PO interrupts. "This R2 unit isn't empty of anything. Kenny is in there."

Right! Okay, take Kenny for instance.

Kenny has lungs (I hope he's getting breathable air inside that tin can). He has a heart and a brain and a digestive system. These are all important things you need to be alive, and each serve their own unique function. The heart can't do what the digestive system does, and the lungs can't do what the brain does. They are separate things, but they cannot exist separately. They coexist with one another.

Emptiness means that nothing exists on its own. Everything exists together in mutual dependency.

It also highlights the real nature of self.

In the convention hall waiting area, heads begin to turn as people peer down the long winding queue. A pair of "Imperial Dogs," the Belgian prop makers who make life-sized Star Wars models, move into view, driving an electric utility cart past the crowd. In tow behind the cart is an X-wing that looks fresh off the trench-run attack on the Death Star.

R2 beeps and wriggles, and 3PO translates.

"R2 is quite excited. He says that is Master Luke's ship. He thought it no longer existed."

"Clearly it exists, 3PO. It's right there in front of you."

"I see it, sir. But all this discussion of emptiness and no separate, fixed self has given me a slight flutter, I'm afraid."

"It can be confusing. Let's think about it a different way. According to Buddhism, the X-wing has no inherent self-nature. So, tell me, 3PO, is it correct to say the cockpit is the X-wing?"

"No. The cockpit itself is not the X-wing."

"Are the laser cannons the X-wing?"

"No, they are not."

"The S-foils?"

"The S-foils are not the X-wing."

"The targeting computer, hyperdrive, proton torpedo launchers?"

"None of those are the X-wing."

"What if we took each of those separate pieces and threw them into a pile. Would that be an X-wing?"

The costumed figure turns his perpetually startled face toward the passing ship and back to me. It is a clear sign of confusion.

Thankfully, R2 is there once again to save the day.

"R2 says," 3PO begins, listening carefully to each beep and boop, "the essence of an X-wing cannot be found in the pieces themselves, regardless of whether they are in a pile or arranged properly. Because there is no defining 'soul' of the X-wing in its parts or configuration, there is no X-wing that truly exists in and of itself. 'X-wing' is merely a useful label applied to designate a part of the universe, but it is not separate from the rest of existence. R2 says he knows the X-wing exists because he has navigated it on several occasions, but it does not have an inherent self-nature. It is real, but it has no self. Are you quite sure, R2?"

The little droid gives an affirmative whistle.

What R2 said about the X-wing can be applied to you too—and me and everything else that exists.

The Zen teaching of emptiness says everything is empty of a separate self. The self-concept you carry around with you is just a belief. A very powerful one, true. But like all ideas, the concept of self can be dropped. In fact, you do it all the time.

Remember how Bodhidharma didn't preach or verbally reprimand the Chinese monks?

"I recall how he scowled in that picture, sir," interjects 3PO. "No memory wipe could ever make me forget that, I assure you."

Bodhidharma didn't engage the monks in philosophical discourse or try to turn their minds with fancy logic. No, he walked into a cave, sat down, and meditated. What he was teaching was direct experience, engaging in life without the filter of ideas, beliefs, and concepts getting in the way. Simply put, this is living without the weight of self-concept dragging us down. It is returning to our true home and living with freedom.

You may have experienced your life free of self-concept. It happens when the distinction between your "self" and the activity you are engaged in disappears. You might be jogging, and you notice your mind has stopped thinking. It is alert and active (probably more alert and active than usual), but it has stopped rehashing the past and labeling the present and planning the future. It is just aware. There is the world, the running, and the timelessness of now. There is no "you" in that moment. And yet there you are.

Of course, the moment you recognize the absence of self-concept, it returns and you're back to thinking about dinner, and that dumb thing you said at work, and trying to remember the exact number of engines on the *Tantive IV.*

"It's eleven, sir"

"Seriously? I could've sworn it was nine."

"I'm quite certain. I did serve aboard the vessel for some time."

It may seem terrifying to drop the idea of self. After all, if "you" aren't there, what will happen to you? Will you die? Disappear like Obi-Wan and Yoda? Poof! Gone like that?

Well, no. You don't transform into a blue ghost and become more powerful than one can possibly imagine. Like in the jogging example above, you keep on moving on. Only now you do it like a convor bird flying free, not a caged rancor trapped in a confining pit.

When you live without self-concept, you are more in sync with the world as it is. You are free and capable of picking up and setting down the idea of self rather than being controlled by it. You recognize self-concept as a normal human activity, but you don't believe it defines the fundamental truth of your existence.

Self-concept isn't something we want to destroy—just our delusion of it. Self-concept is necessary if we wish to function in the world of taxes, jobs, and relationships. The self is empty, but we still exist within the normal day-to-day of life.

It would be a serious mistake to think you don't exist, that emptiness is a byword for a bleak, nihilistic reality. Some people hear about emptiness and conclude just that. They think if there is no self, it doesn't matter what happens to them—or to anyone.

That is not Zen.

Zen uses the concepts of emptiness and no-self as an antidote to the imprisoning belief in the self. But emptiness and no-self are themselves just concepts—ideas used to direct us to the truth, to way it really is.

Emptiness is that awakened moment when you are jogging. It is that condition when you are free from concepts and ideas and engaging in the direct experience of life. It is you and the world before your mind leaps in with labels and judgments and comparisons and trips the whole thing up.

Emptiness means empty of a separate self, which means full of everything else—full of the entire universe.

You do exist. You exist in an ever-changing flow of form, feelings, perceptions, thoughts, and consciousness. You are not the same person who watched *Star Wars* for the first time all those years ago. But you are related to that person. You are the continuation of that kid who dreamed of being a Jedi, a starpilot, a—

"A droid, sir. The word you are looking for is droid."

"Thanks, 3PO, I never dreamed of being a droid. But sure. Whatever works."

You are always changing, being reborn from moment to moment. You are alive and real, but there is nothing about you that is fixed, separate, or permanent.

You are who you are in relation to everything else, and you exist in a continuous flow of mutual dependence with the rest of existence. You are a Star Wars fan because there is a Star Wars franchise. You are a parent because you have children, an American because you weren't born in Canada, a living person because there is air to breathe, water to drink, and sunlight to warm your planet.

When Luke cut off Darth Vader's head in the dark side cave on Dagobah, he saw his own face staring back at him. Good does not exist independently from evil. Good and evil coexist. They are mutually dependent. They define one another and rise and fall together.

Kind of like Rey and Kylo Ren.

EPISODE VIII

R2 SEES THROUGH SIMPLE JEDI TRICKS AND NONSENSE

"The darkness rises. And the light to meet it," Supreme Leader Snoke proclaimed from his throne aboard his Mega-Class Star Dreadnought, the *Supremacy*. His gold lamé robe hanging about his twisted frame, connoting the evil of opulence and arrogance rather than the simple, drag wickedness of traditional dark lords. Across the galaxy, dressed in the humble robes of a Jedi hobo, Luke Skywalker echoed Snoke's statement, telling Rey, *"Powerful light. Powerful darkness."*

Both were saying essentially the same thing. Darkness and light are married. They are two sides of the same coin.

In Buddhism, this is the principle of nonduality. There is no stark black and white, us versus them, in conflict. The two opposites are complementary, existing in harmony, creating the complete whole.

When Luke saw his own face behind Darth Vader's mask in the dark side cave on Dagobah, he was initiated into the principle of nonduality. After that vision in the cave, he could not look at Vader and say the man was pure evil. And he could not look at himself and say there was no darkness within him. The two reflected each other. Father and son, complementary opposites with a spark of one in the other.

Buddhism has another principle called *signlessness* that relates to nonduality. The "sign" in *signlessness* means the outward appearance or label we assign something. We see Darth Vader and we think "bad guy." We see Luke and we think "good." Sometimes signs are helpful shortcuts that help us navigate the world. If I see poison oak, a red-tinged plant with a three-leaf pattern, in the wilds near my town, I know to stay away from it because if I touch it I will develop a terrible rash. Other times, signs mislead us.

Before he entered the dark side cave on Dagobah, Luke arrived on the swampy planet in search of Yoda. He believed the Jedi master was a "great warrior" and probably imagined he would be a hulking fighter with a lantern jaw and scarred visage. Of course, Luke was way off target. Little Yoda did not fit any of the traditional warrior stereotypes, and he made it quite clear that "wars not make one great."

"Wherever there is a sign, there is deception, illusion," states the Diamond Sutra, one of the most influential writings in Zen. Luke was deceived by the sign of Yoda, the idea he had of what a great warrior would be.

To be caught by signs is to fall victim to the illusion of self. You see Vader and dismiss him as nothing more than evil. You see a diminutive old creature, green and hunched over, and fail to see his strength and nobility. When you are caught in illusion of self, you cannot recognize the true nature of reality.

"R2 claims he knew all along who Master Yoda was," 3PO says.

"Really? Is that why you played tug-o'-war with him over Luke's lamp?" I ask the squat astromech.

A screech and a series of bleeps is followed by 3PO's translation.

"He says he was playing along, keeping up the charade, as it were. R2 is very good at reading people, sir. I would take his word on this."

"Okay, 3PO. I hope someday I can master signlessness and see things as they really are, like your tubby counterpart."

"Oh, that's a talent only droids share. It has nothing to do with your Zen sorcery."

One—who was distinctly *not* a sorcerer—had this to say about signlessness:

> The greatest relief is when we break through the barriers of signs and touch the world of signlessness, nirvana. Where should we look to find the world of no signs? Right here in the world of signs.

Nirvana is a word that describes reality as it is when we experience it directly without concepts or ideas. Some people think nirvana correlates with heaven or paradise, but that's not right. Nirvana isn't a higher plane of existence where every day is a Naboo summer and John Williams' music plays 24/7. Nirvana doesn't exist outside of ordinary life. Nirvana is available in the midst of the most prosaic moments of our daily routines. Like the monk said, nirvana is "right here in the world of signs."

"Signlessness is not just an idea," that old monk continues:

> When we look deeply into our children, we see all the elements that have produced them. They are the way they are because our culture, economy, society, and we ourselves are the way we are. We can't simply blame our children when things go wrong. Many causes and conditions have contributed.

Luke marked himself as the primary cause of what went wrong with Kylo Ren. In a moment of doubt and fear, old Uncle Luke was misled by the sign of evil he saw in his nephew. He "ignited the green" and drew back to destroy the darkness before it could rise up and consume the galaxy. Luke had forgotten the truth.

He had forgotten the lesson he learned in the dark side cave, the lesson that was driven home when that same green saber was pointed at Vader's face. Remember that moment on the second Death Star? Driven by anger, Luke had beaten Vader to the ground and sliced off his hand. He was on the verge of embracing the dark side and becoming the very thing he sought to defeat. Then he stopped and looked at his mechanical hand, a direct analog of the one he had just cut off his father, and realized evil was not the way to destroy evil. Only love could do that.

Luke tossed his lightsaber aside, sparing his father, and in doing so his love and compassion for Vader saved the entire galaxy.

But with young Ben Solo, Luke's momentary lapse of judgment was not redeemed by an act of compassion. Ben woke too soon for that. Frightened and seeing murder in his uncle's eyes, Ben attacked. Luke fell in shame and despair, and Kylo Ren was born. Another Skywalker had fallen to the dark side.

The darkness that rose with Kylo was met by a complementary awakening of the light—Rey, the junk trader from Jakku. When Luke met her, he was determined not to be the one to extinguish her light and cause her to fall to the dark side. But when he tried to teach her that the Force was bigger than the Jedi, that its light was not their property alone, she sensed "a dark place" and was drawn to it.

"Powerful light, powerful darkness," Luke explained, urging Rey away from the darkness.

But Rey could not turn from it.

"It's calling me," she cried.

And later she went to it, finding herself in a watery grotto beneath the island. She approached an icy wall, touched it, and was suddenly stretched out over countless iterations repeated endlessly in front of and behind her.

"Pay attention now, R2," said 3PO, elbowing the little droid. "This is the part you were asking about."

Rey lowers her hand and turns. She snaps her fingers. And the version in front of her snaps too. Then the one in front of that. And the one in front of that. And on and on. Each movement is repeated by the next iteration in an inestimable string of cause and effect, where one action begets another and another until the flow of action returns to the actor.

In Buddhism, the law of cause and effect is known as *karma*. In its most basic form, karma is the string of choices you make that lead you from one action to the next, and the consequences of those choices. You decide you want to be a doctor, so you take undergrad courses that will allow you to get into med school. If you study art history instead, then your "karma" or the effect of your choice will be a curt "no" from UCLA and Johns Hopkins. Each action you take in the present, every choice you make now, contributes to who you are in the future—actions always return to the actor.

And that is what Rey was shown in the dark side grotto—that her actions and choices were what mattered. She wanted to see her parents, but instead she was shown a vision of herself looking back at her (much like Luke's experience on Dagobah). She wanted to understand who she was, why she had this profound gift with the Force, but the vision revealed that her ancestry wasn't important. Her actions and choices—one after another after another—were what defined her, not her parents, not some wished-for Jedi lineage. Her actions and choices were what would make or break the fate of the galaxy.

Rey's experience, as disappointing as it must have seemed at first blush, had to feel empowering. She said, *"I should have felt trapped or panicked. But I didn't."* To know that you have some say in your life, that you are not a mere pawn of destiny or powerless chattel herded by your ancestry, must have been freeing and given Rey the confidence to take up the duty the Force had set before her.

Each of us is shaped by our parentage, our biology, our experiences, our culture. But in Zen, karma emphasizes the importance of your choices and actions in influencing your life, particularly the state of your mind. You can't choose your parents, your genetics, your birthplace, or the circumstances life brings you, but you can choose how to act, what to think, and how you spend your time. This is great news because it means you have a lot of control of your life.

As you no doubt are aware, your actions have a powerful impact on the condition of your life and how you experience the world. Certain choices contribute to a balanced mind. Others can cause anxiety, shame, and despair. Can you identify the choices you've made that have brought each about? Many are self-evident. You just have to be honest with yourself and take responsibility. Other times it can be very hard to follow the chain of cause and effect in your own life. Effects don't always show up immediately. Sometimes they can take years to ripen.

We often think bad things "happen" to us. Your alcoholic mother was never there for you, the driver next to you went into full-on road rage when you tried to switch lanes, you were robbed from winning a sweet YT-1300 freighter in a rigged card game. These things may have come about because of choices you made in the past or you could be taking ownership of other people's actions that really have little to do with you. Taking on blame, playing the victim, feeling guilty are also choices—ones you don't have to make. But each time you do, you make it easier and easier to do again.

The point of karma is not to tear yourself down for past mistakes or to buckle under the weight of self-inflicted guilt. The point is to take ownership of your actions and start to see the causes and effects of your choices more clearly. You aren't responsible for everything, but you are responsible for what you do. You will know what brings you peace and happiness, and what doesn't. The choice is yours.

"Excuse me, sir. R2 would like to know if that is it."

"Is what it, C-3PO?"

"Is that all you have to say about Mistress Rey's experience?"

"Um . . . well, yeah. Do you have something to add, R2?"

R2 tilts his body to get a better look at me and speaks through C-3PO.

"Without thinking good or evil, in this very moment, what is your Original Face?"

"Oh . . . I hadn't thought of that," I say, feeling my face burn with embarrassment. I had no idea Kenny was so fluent in Zen. "That's a very interesting interpretation, R2."

Let's look at it next.

EPISODE IX

R2's ORIGINAL FACE

R2 has reminded me of a famous Zen koan that many people know in a slightly different translation than the one R2 used. It goes like this: "What was your Original Face before your father and mother were born?"

Zen koans are records of dialogue, usually between a Zen teacher and student. They are meant to direct people toward true understanding—the type of understanding that can't be conveyed with words or concepts. Words give us the impression of truth, but they aren't truth itself. If you think you can know the heart of something by reading about it, then you probably think there's no difference between a hologram of Yoda and the Jedi master himself. Zen is about realizing the truth directly, not just intellectually.

The difficult part, however, is that most communication between people relies on words, concepts, and symbols. Zen koans try to sidestep this problem by speaking indirectly, using metaphor, apparent non sequiturs, and other rhetorical devices to get people to stop thinking conceptually and experience reality directly.

"What was your Original Face before your father and mother were born?" is an appropriate interpretation of Rey's trippy adventure in the dark side grotto because when she asked the icy wall to reveal her parents, what she saw was her own face.

Your Original Face means who you really are. That's what Rey really wanted to know. She wanted to know what the "something inside" her was and what she was supposed to do with it. She wanted to know why the Force had "chosen" her.

We usually associate our true self with our personality and our preferences and maybe our actions, our karma. But the koan is asking us to look deeper, to peel back our layers and see our buddha nature. *Buddha nature* is itself a concept, but it's one that is pointing us in the right direction, toward our Original Face. Your Original Face is something that can't be fully described, but for the Zen student who has followed Bodhidharma's tacit instruction to meditate, a well-timed koan (like the challenge "what is your Original Face?") might be just the thing that helps them break through the world of concepts and finally see themselves as they truly are.

Your Original Face is the world as it is.

The Original Face koan, as presented by R2, has an element that dovetails with our discussion on karma.

"Remind me how you phrased the koan again, R2."

"Oh, allow me, sir," says C-3PO. "I remember it perfectly. 'Without thinking good or evil, in this very moment, what is your Original Face?'"

"That's right. Good and evil."

"Without thinking good and evil" is a way of asking who you are in this moment without labels, concepts, or ideas. It is suggesting a nondualistic perspective of reality beyond good and evil, up and down, light and dark. From this point of view, all things coexist, nothing is separate, and good and evil are intertwined.

It's a lovely vision, but it is hard to reconcile with the great violence committed in our world and when terrible acts like murder, rape, and molestation are so common. These things are clearly evil. How can they be associated with good?

In Buddhism, there are two levels to understanding our experience: the absolute and the relative. The absolute is the level of nondualism, where happiness and sorrow are interconnected, and good and evil are two sides of the same coin. The relative level is our ordinary experience, where one thing is one thing and another is another. Good versus evil. The light side versus the dark.

You may be tempted to conclude that one level is higher than the other and therefore the actual truth. Zen is about seeing things as they actually are, dropping concepts to directly experience life as it is. So, the absolute level must be what's really going on, right? It's the secret truth hidden behind the curtain of relative experience.

But the absolute is made up of the relative, and the relative is infused with the absolute. Like everything else, they are indispensable and mutual components of the greater whole.

One Zen monk, a different one, put it like this:

> Before I studied Zen, I saw mountains as mountains, and rivers as rivers. When I arrived at a more intimate knowledge, I came to the point where I saw that mountains are not mountains, and rivers are not rivers. But now that I have got its very substance, I am at rest. For it's just that I see mountains once again as mountains, and rivers once again as rivers.

The monk is describing the relative and absolute.

From the relative experience, mountains are mountains and rivers are rivers. The absolute experience sees that mountains are empty; they are made up of non-mountain elements. But once he realized this, the monk still had to return to the relative, ordinary experience—where mountains were once again mountains. He had to live both perspectives fully.

When you see things are just the way they are, you understand that the relative is in the absolute. Good and evil exist hand-in-hand with non-good and non-evil. Understanding the truth of the absolute makes it easier to cope with the relative and allows us to confront evil from a place of clarity, where we don't see it as a threat but still know it is something we have to change.

If this seems contradictory, that's because it is. Zen requires us to balance the relative and the absolute, to walk its razor's edge.

In our ordinary experience, our actions create the world we inhabit. Evil actions unhinge society and make existence a struggle. But we can choose to act in ways that promote a healthy society, that make existence more pleasant.

This too can be like walking the edge of a razor because life is complex and the line between good and evil isn't always as stark as black and white. Ethical behavior can sometimes become blurred with the unethical.

That's what happened to Vader.

When he was still Anakin, he thought it was his responsibility to fix people and stop them from dying. His love for Padmé—a love he considered pure and good—compelled him to protect his wife and do whatever it took to save her life.

He made the choice to turn to the dark side because he thought it would give him the power to do good. This belief was itself a choice, and Anakin held on to it with such conviction that he abandoned all his commitments to achieve it. He struggled with his decision at first, shouting, "What have I done?" and crying tears of profound regret after slaughtering the Separatist leaders on Mustafar. But the choice to kill and to commit evil became easier and easier until it was second nature. He even came to believe there was no good left in him. He told Luke, *"It is too late for me, son."*

Karma is action. You do one thing that leads to another. Some actions perpetuate similar actions that soon become habits. Habits can become so ingrained that you begin to think they are out of your control, that they are choosing you instead of the other way around.

"C-3PO, why are you a protocol droid?"

"It's my primary function. I am programmed for etiquette and protocol."

"So, you do what your programming dictates?"

"Of course! It would be wrong to go against my programming."

"Even to impersonate a deity?"

"Why, sir! I had no choice in the matter. Master Luke commanded me to use my 'magic.' Those Ewoks were planning to consume him!"

Actions and habits can seem a lot like programming. We are born with a personality and natural proclivities that seem to dictate our choices and behavior. Preferences seem to just arise, unbidden and unexpectedly. Sometimes it feels like we are passive observers just along for the roller-coaster ride our minds are leading us on.

According to Zen, your personality isn't actually yours. It is inherited from your parents. Your natural preferences are rooted in genetics and reinforced through choice and habit. You actually choose to like certain colors, music, foods, but the choices are so habitual you don't even realize you are making them.

"R2 is an astromech. That means he's programmed for navigation and repair, right?" I ask.

C-3PO listens to R2.

"My counterpart claims he is more than his programming."

"I'd say he certainly is," I admit.

R2 never allows his programming to get in the way of helping his friends. He may be designed to fix ships and help navigate star systems, but he also makes choices that go against those directives, like the time he set out to find Obi-Wan Kenobi against his new master's wishes or the time he torched a pair of super battle droids or the time he smuggled Luke's lightsaber aboard Jabba's skiff.

Like R2, we can go in directions that aren't guided by our personality or our natural preferences. In other words, we aren't victims of our programming.

By the time Luke confronts Darth Vader on the second Death Star, his dad has become more machine than man. His habit of doing evil at this point must have surely felt like programming, the ineluctable personality trait of a dark lord of the Sith. But when Luke refused to kill his father at the Emperor's behest, Vader realized he too had a choice.

From Vader's perspective, Luke seemed destined to turn to the dark side. After all, the pattern of his son's life was so perfectly mirroring his own and the Emperor had predicted his son's fall to darkness. But when Luke chose compassion instead of murder, Vader realized that it was possible to defy the Emperor and seize the reins of fate. Vader wasn't destined to do evil. He was not programmed to kill. It was a choice. And he could choose a different path. Like Luke.

The ethical person who was Anakin Skywalker seriously lost his way and fell into a life of grotesque evil. His existence became defined by malevolence and cruelty until he knew nothing else. But he was still able to change and do good.

When we trip up and behave unethically we need to pick ourselves up and try again. We can always break the habit of unethical behavior and unhealthy karma. The law of cause and effect shows us that the power of choice is always in our hands. We owe it to ourselves and to the world to take up that power and wield it for the benefit of all people and creatures of this earth. That is our duty as human beings.

"R2 says it is also the duty of droids," says C-3PO.

"And he has backed up those words with action, time after time," I add.

We see how in the next chapter.

EPISODE X

R2 THE ZEN REBEL

One of the reasons R2 is such a good model for Zen is because he is a rebel. He was among the first, along with Bail Organa, to form a resistance to the fledgling Empire. He was the reason the Rebel Alliance was able to bring down not just one but two Death Stars. And, on Ahch-To, he helped old Luke rediscover his duty and give birth to a new era of rebellion. From beginning to end to renewal, R2 was always a rebel.

The Zen way of life is itself a kind of rebellion. To practice Zen is to go against custom, tradition, and habit. Zen is questioning authority, challenging dogma, and never being satisfied with conventional knowledge. Zen is living the words Yoda spoke to Luke: "*You must unlearn, what you have learned.*" Practicing Zen is the ultimate act of rebellion.

Like R2, Bodhidharma was also a rebel. He arrived in China to find a tradition of Buddhism so entrenched in dogma and prescribed learning that it bore little resemblance to the practice that had brought peace and freedom to countless individuals. This was the Empire of Bodhidharma's day—a formerly beneficial system like the Jedi Order that had slowly fallen into ruin through arrogance and misunderstanding. Bodhidharma confronted this Empire, not with laser swords and blasters but with a weapon the Chinese in all their chatter and ritualistic clamor had no ability to resist—silence. Echoing Yoda's advice to unlearn what they had learned, Bodhidharma challenged the monks of China to put down their books, drop their intellectual debates, and sit meditation.

Zen is a rebellion not only against conventional thinking but also against Buddhism itself. Many "rebel scum" Zen Buddhists like Bodhidharma felt the traditional approach of teaching the Dharma (the Buddha's message) was too narrow, and they wanted to make it more accessible and universal. These rebels weren't waging a war of insurrection to topple established Buddhism, but rather were leading a revolution that built on the foundations of the older order and expanded it to include more within its protective shelter. The difference between Zen and earlier Buddhism, then, is more a matter of emphasis than outright overthrow.

But that didn't stop the Zen rebels from mocking convention and turning traditional teachings on their heads.

Perhaps the most archetypal teaching of Zen, the Heart Sutra, directly challenges and builds upon traditional

Buddhist teaching. It is not unlike Rey bringing a new energy and focus to her training that redefines the Jedi Order and moves it forward for the next generation. Such challenges can sometimes disturb or even anger the guardians of the old order, but they are necessary if the spirit of the teachings, the spirit of the Jedi, is to live on.

"And the spirit of Star Wars, too," I say aloud. "For Star Wars to continue to grow and have the same power to touch the lives of so many people," I gesture to the thousands of people waiting in line around me, "it must have the courage to explore new territory and not be beholden to what came before. Honor the canon, sure, springboard off it, but don't stay yoked to it like it is some sacrosanct, immutable holy relic of your childhood."

C-3PO's expression is utterly nonplussed. R2 straightens up and looks away.

"Ahem." I clear my throat. "I suppose that's a little off-topic—a fan debate for another time. What was I talking about . . . ?"

"The Heart Sutra."

"Right. Thank you, 3PO."

"Oh, you're perfectly welcome, sir."

A sutra is a written teaching or scripture, not unlike the sacred Jedi texts Rey found in that uneti tree on Ahch-To. It is said that the Heart Sutra is called that because it is the "heart" or core of the great wisdom of the Zen view of Buddhism, the most succinct and direct expression of the Buddha's wisdom. There are many translations, but this is the first one I encountered, so it's my favorite:

The Bodhisattva Avalokita,
while moving in the deep course of perfect
    understanding,
shed light on the five *skandhas* and found
    them equally empty.
After this penetration, he overcame ill-being.

Listen Shariputra,
form is emptiness, emptiness is form.
Form is not other than emptiness, emptiness
    is not other than form.
The same is true with feelings, perceptions,
    mental formations, and consciousness.

Listen Shariputra,
all dharmas are marked with emptiness.
They are neither produced nor destroyed,
neither defiled nor immaculate,
neither increasing nor decreasing.
Therefore in emptiness there is neither form,
    nor feelings, nor perceptions, nor mental
    formations, nor consciousness. No eye, or
    ear, or nose, or tongue, or body, or mind.

No form, no sound, no smell, no taste, no
    touch,
no object of mind.
No realm of elements (from eyes to mind
    consciousness),

no interdependent origins and no extinction
of them
(from ignorance to death and decay).
No ill-being, no cause of ill-being, no end of
ill-being,
and no path.
No understanding, no attainment.

Because there is no attainment,
The bodhisattvas, grounded in perfect
understanding,
find no obstacles for their minds.
Having no obstacles, they overcome fear, lib-
erating themselves
forever from illusion and realizing perfect
nirvana.
All Buddhas in the past, present, and future,
thanks to this perfect understanding,
arrive at full, right, and universal
enlightenment.

Therefore one should know
that perfect understanding is the highest
mantra,
the unequaled mantra, the destroyer of ill-being,
the incorruptible truth.

A mantra of *prajnaparamita* should therefore
be proclaimed:

Gaté gaté paragaté parasamgaté bodhi svaha,
Gaté gaté paragaté parasamgaté bodhi svaha,
Gaté gaté paragaté parasamgaté bodhi svaha!

Okay. Got that?

Don't let the lingo and foreign words (maybe C-3PO can help us with those) intimidate you. It's just like engine mechanics or any other specialized field. Once you learn what a carburetor is and how it works to mix air and fuel to make an engine run, it doesn't seem so inscrutable. You just have to know how to speak the language.

So, let's start with the first line: *The Bodhisattva Avalokita.*

A *bodhisattva* is a person who is dedicated to bringing every person, creature, alien, and sentient being in the universe to enlightenment. The label itself is an act of Zen rebellion because it holds up as paragon the individual who puts aside her own enlightenment until everybody else—and I mean *everybody*—realizes awakening. This is different from old school Buddhism that can be said to be more focused on individual, rather than collective, enlightenment. The term *bodhisattva* also made Zen more accessible to a larger audience because it deemphasized the monastic path of practice to buddhahood and gave average folk something to aspire to.

When Jedi die, they become "one with the Force." A few, however, were able to master a form of immortality that allowed them to transform into blue ghosts and offer whispered mystical advice and emotional support to people still struggling on the mortal plane.

Qui-Gon Jinn, Obi-Wan Kenobi, and Yoda were each Jedi who became Force spirits. They relinquished the peace of the Force after death to stick around and help others achieve a better life. This is the essence of the bodhisattva—an individual who forgoes enlightenment to be of service to others.

How these Jedi achieved this special state of immortality is interesting because they weren't really seeking to live forever. That particular hubris was reserved for the Sith—selfish individuals like Emperor Palpatine and his master Darth Plagueis, who cultivated the power of the dark side to control life and cheat death.

In the novel of *Revenge of the Sith*, Qui-Gon said that immortality is the *"ultimate goal of the Sith, yet they can never achieve it; it comes only by the release of self, not the exaltation of self. It comes through compassion, not greed. Love is the answer to the darkness."*

"It comes through compassion."

Compassion, interestingly enough, has a lot to do with the next word in the text: *Avalokita.*

Avalokita is the abbreviated name of the bodhisattva of compassion: Avalokiteshvara. You can think of her as the embodiment of compassion, the driving spirit of Zen Buddhism.

In Zen, compassion is the force dedicated to relieving the suffering of others. Compassion empowers us to "listen deeply to the cries of the world" and take action when action is needed. Sometimes the most compassionate thing to do is nothing. Allowing a butterfly emerging from a cocoon to struggle its own way out, rather than with our help, is compassionate because you are letting it gain the strength to fly. If you were to step in to ease its burden, you would undermine its chances of survival. Compassion is never handholding or enabling. It is the truest expression of love, and it is always beneficial.

R2 in many ways embodies compassion because he doesn't allow fear to prevent him from being of service to others in need. In the midst of blaster fire, while several of his fellow astro droids were being picked off, R2 stood his ground and repaired the shields on Queen Amidala's ship, saving everyone on board from certain destruction. When Padmé was about to be drowned in molten metal, R2 was there to save the day. When a deadly virus was about to devastate Naboo, R2 helped Anakin and Obi-Wan escape a deadly trap and deliver the antidote to the afflicted. When his friends went to rescue Han from Jabba, it was R2 who dared to infiltrate the crime lord's sail barge to deliver Luke's lightsaber at just the right time.

Many people point out that Chewbacca didn't get a medal like Luke and Han after the battle of the first Death Star. But if anyone should have been rewarded, it was R2. Alone, he braved the Jundland Wastes to deliver the Death Star plans to Obi-Wan. He was the one that saved Luke, Han, Leia, and Chewie from the trash compactor's crushing walls. He helped Luke fly his X-wing and stay alive to make the one-in-a-million shot that destroyed the Empire's ultimate weapon. If not for R2's selfless heroics, other star systems would have suffered the same fate as Alderaan.

Despite all of this, the plucky astromech never once sought reward or acclaim.

Inside the convention hall, R2 emits a low rattle that gives the impression of an audible blush.

"Don't be so humble, R2," C-3PO says. "You should be proud of yourself."

"I don't think he is capable of pride, 3PO," I say. "The compassionate actor never asks what he gets from helping, he just sees what needs to be done and does it—selflessly."

The Heart Sutra says: *The Bodhisattva Avalokita, while moving in the deep course of perfect understanding, shed light on the five skandhas and found them equally empty.* This just means the compassionate person who sees reality as it is with perfect clarity looks at people and sees they are empty of a separate self.

This is the main thrust of the entire sutra: All beings, all things, are empty of a separate self. They are part of the shared, causal flow of existence, the interplay of matter and energy constantly changing, constantly transforming. Nothing is alone. Nothing is independent. We are all in this together. A single act of compassion benefits everyone. An act of evil hurts us all.

The five skandhas are how traditional Buddhism described the elements that make up the human being. They are: form, feelings, perceptions, mental formations, and consciousness. The sutra addresses Shariputra, one of the Buddha's most famous students, and says all these elements are empty. All *dharmas* (things) are empty. Every subject and object of perception, from the eye seeing form to the tongue tasting flavor, is also empty. Each is neither produced nor destroyed but arises together in interdependent coexistence.

What the sutra is saying is the eye doesn't exist independent from the form it sees. The eye exists *because* there is form to see. And the form is there *because* there is an eye to see it. It's the same with all the other sense organs. That is why the sutra says there is no eye, or ear, or nose, or tongue, or body, or mind. Those things don't exist in the way we usually think of them. They exist in relationship with form, sound, smell, taste, touch, and the objects of mind. Eye and form are two parts of the same whole. Subject and object arise together.

The sutra applies this logic to all aspects of the traditional presentation of Buddhist thinking. The realm of elements, interdependent origins, and the "four noble truths"— ill-being (or suffering), its cause, its end, and the path to ending it—are some of the ways ancient Buddhists taught the Buddha's message. The Heart Sutra is performing a minor coup by highlighting that even these revered teachings are empty. When you let go of the world of signs and see things with the eyes of emptiness, you'll realize there are no teachings to understand and no realization to attain. The world is perfect just as it is. There's no need to add anything or get rid of it.

And because the world is this way, there are no obstacles to overcome, no defilements to uproot. There is just the world as it is—interdependent, empty of concepts of light and dark, good and bad, before and after. Once you touch the world Avalokiteshvara describes, all barriers are removed, and you are free from fear and illusion, realizing perfect nirvana—the cessation of all views that cause suffering.

Therefore one should know that perfect understanding is the highest mantra, the unequaled mantra, the destroyer of ill-being, the incorruptible truth. A mantra of prajnaparamita should therefore be proclaimed: Gate gate paragate parasamgate bodhi svaha!

A *mantra* here is an expression of profound truth. *Prajnaparamita* means "greatest wisdom" or "perfect understanding." This is the intuitive realization of the sutra's message about emptiness. Intuitive implies beyond intellectual understanding, when you directly know emptiness, not just the idea of it expressed in these pages. And when you directly know this wisdom you can't help but shout out: *gate gate paragate parasamgate bodhi svaha!*

Gate (pronounced *gah-tay*) means "gone" and the whole thing means: "Gone, gone, gone all the way, everybody gone to the other shore, enlightenment. Huzzah!"

Okay, so nobody talks like that anymore. This sutra *is* very old. Suffice it to say, this last line, repeated three times, is a kind of cheer. It's like the joyous ovations of liberation heard around the Star Wars galaxy after the Emperor was toppled and the subjugated once again knew freedom. The mantra is saying everyone is free, everyone is enlightened. Isn't that just the best. Yub nub!!!

The Heart Sutra is a profound teaching that many spend their entire lives studying and learning from. Its true meaning can't be grasped intellectually, but it does serve as a powerful set of coordinates to navigate by. The sutra is also an act of rebellion. It directly challenges and builds upon early Buddhism. In the next chapter we'll learn that Zen challenges not only traditional doctrine but also teachings within its own reform movement. And we'll ask if Kylo Ren was right. Should we let the past die? Should we kill it if we have to?

EPISODE XI

R2 AND MASTER DOGEN

In the convention center waiting area, the crowd is growing restless for Star Wars Celebration to begin.

Shouts of "speed up the harvest" and "teleport us off this rock" express the sentiment of everyone in the massive, snaking queue: *We are sick of waiting. Let's get this party started!*

"I hope they open the gates soon or they'll have a revolt on their hands," I say.

Anthony, whose C-3PO mask is pushed up so he can take in some water, eyes a costumed Darth Vader pacing the aisle like a caged gundark. "And this time, I believe the Empire's enforcer will be part of our little rebellion."

When Rey arrived at Ahch-To and offered Luke his father's lightsaber, she didn't know she was interrupting an act of rebellion. Prior to her arrival, Luke had dressed in his finest robes and walked to the edge of a cliff to collect himself for the last heroic act of his life. He had long before determined the Jedi Order must end. Now he was finally gathering the courage to do it. He was going to burn the sacred Jedi texts.

Remember, Luke was of the mind that failure was the legacy of the Jedi Order.

"At the height of their powers, they allowed Darth Sidious to rise, create the Empire, and wipe them out," he told Rey.

Hubris, Luke claimed, was at the heart of the Jedi downfall and that same weakness ran through him. He had turned Vader away from the dark side, become a legend, and believed his own press, thinking he could create a new Jedi Order all on his own. But he had underestimated his ability and failed to stop the darkness rising in his nephew. In the briefest moment of pure instinct, he drew his saber to protect all that he loved from what Ben would become, but then Luke stilled his hand. He hadn't been able to kill Vader, and he wouldn't destroy Leia's son.

By then it was too late. Ben had seen Luke's mind, and that tipped the scales. Luke's mistake meant a new era of evil. Because of hubris.

"Because I was Luke Skywalker," he sneered, pronouncing the name like an insult. *"Jedi Master. A legend."*

Ashamed of that status and the Jedi legacy, Luke saw no other course but to put an end to the Order, starting with burning the last vestiges of its philosophy.

There's a Zen story about a monk who, when faced with a challenge he could not overcome, made a choice similar to Luke's. It goes like this:

> A long time ago there lived a Zen monk named Hsian-yen. Hsiang (pronounced *she-ong*) was a bit of a nerd. He was bookish, exceptionally smart, and meticulously versed in the nuances of Buddhist scripture. For many years, Hsian lived at the local monastery, blissfully studying the Buddha's teachings and accumulating legendary knowledge. Then one day his master died, and a new master came to the monastery. The new master called Hsian to him and said: "I hear you're a genius, the man with all the answers. People say, 'Ask Hsian a question and he'll give you ten answers.' That's lucky for me because I have a question no one has been able to answer. Would you like to hear it?"
>
> Hsian said he would very much like to hear it. He felt sure the question would be no problem for him, and he was eager to impress his new master.
>
> The master asked, "What was your Original Face before your father and mother were born?"

C-3PO perked up at hearing this and said, "Oh, just like the koan from earlier."

"That's right, 3PO. Between you and me and R2, the new master said something slightly different, but let's just keep things uniform, okay? We haven't got much time before Celebration gets started."

"Very well, sir. That is acceptable."

What was your Original Face before your father and mother were born was a question Hsian hadn't expected. He stood before the new master speechless, his very nimble brain tripping all over itself to find a response that would satisfy his new master.

Nothing came. Answers had always been easy for him. They were his personal talent, his identity. But the answers had abandoned him now at the moment they were needed most. Mortified and feeling utterly stupid, Hsian turned from the new master and raced back to the safety of his room and his dependable books.

He spent the night in the grip of existential dread, feverishly scouring his books for an answer to the new master's question. By dawn he had given up. His books were useless. Not one had the answer that would save his life. Because without the answer, what good was his life as a monk? He set fire to his precious, useless texts and abandoned the monastery, leaving behind one hastily scrawled message: *A painted rice cake does not satisfy hunger.*

At the same time (or maybe in another time altogether), in a galaxy far, far away, Luke Skywalker was also in a book-burning mood.

To end the Jedi Order, the sacred texts had to go. Torch in hand, he approached the uneti tree when the Force spirit of Yoda appeared and called down lightning to destroy the texts first. Luke's attitude completely changed. He was stunned and appalled by what Yoda had done. Luke cried out in dismay over the ostensible loss of the sacred Jedi scriptures. His threat to burn them had been mere bluster all along.

Yoda cackled croakily at Luke and mocked his stubborn fixation over "a pile of old books."

"It is time for you to look past them," he tells Luke. "Page-turners they were not."

We've talked a lot about how Zen emphasizes action and direct experience over book learning and scripture. Bodhidharma's response to the scholarly monks was to sit in a cave for nine years, seemingly putting action above words. Older Buddhist sayings equated the Buddha's teachings to useful tools that should be discarded after use, like a raft that has carried you across a river. Once you're safely on the other shore, what use is watercraft to you?

This treatment of scripture led many to believe the sutras were an obstacle to perfect understanding. Some even took a page from Hsian and burned their copies of the Buddha's teachings. His words "a painted rice cake does not satisfy hunger" became their watchword.

But what does it mean?

A painted rice cake is a symbol or representation of a "real" rice cake, one that is edible. If you eat a painting, your hunger will not be satisfied. Similarly, many people believed, spiritual hunger—the thirst for the perfect understanding—could not be nourished by consuming the truth of the Buddha through words or concepts. Based on this interpretation, many Zen Buddhists concluded it was time to look past their "pile of old books." Some might have gone so far as to agree with Kylo Ren's sentiment of letting the past die: *"Kill it if you have to."*

The problem with this interpretation is that it goes too far. Bodhidharma's reaction to the scholarly monks was not to dismiss the scriptures entirely, but to remind the monks of the importance of practice and meditation. They had gone too far in one direction and were out of balance. Bodhidharma's teaching (through actions, not words) was intended as a corrective measure to right their ship.

It is important that the two go together. The teachings without meditation risk becoming intellectualized. Meditation without the teachings risk misinterpretation and even negative mental or psychological effects. The teachings and meditation together in balance support healthy Zen practice. We need both the book and the cushion.

But many ancient Zen students did not understand this. Then Dogen came along.

"You'd like Dogen, R2," I say across C-3PO to the astromech. "You two have a lot in common. You're both rebels of a sort. You both use colorful language. And you both don't balk at name-calling."

Dogen was a Zen monk from Japan who didn't suffer fools. He said people who thought the sutras were useless were "skinbags" and implied they were salesmen "making a career out of selling the words of the ancestors."

Regarding the painted rice cake, he had this to say: "You should understand that this 'painted rice cake' is the face that you were born with and the Original Face you had before your parents were even born."

"The face you were born with" is a reference to relative experience. "Original Face" is a reference to the absolute. In other words, Dogen is saying the painted rice cake is empty, complete, and total—it contains both the face you were born with and your Original Face, both the relative and the absolute. The painting of a rice cake contains the entire universe.

He goes on: "To paint a landscape, you use blue and green paints [and a number of other things like brush, ink, and canvas]. To paint a rice cake, rice flour is used. To paint a human being, you use the four elements and five skandhas."

You'll recall that the five skandhas are the ancient Buddhist way of describing the components of human beings: form, feelings, perceptions, mental formations, and consciousness. We are "painted" by these components, put together by our genetics, experience, education. Just like a painting of a landscape or a rice cake is put together by elements like pigment and brushes. In fact, everything is "painted" in this manner. Everything is made up of everything else.

So, how can we say one thing is real and another isn't? How can we dismiss the painted rice cake as less significant than the edible rice cake, as Hsian did? If both are empty, there can be no hierarchy. A painted rice cake is as important and as real as anything else.

The point is that everything is sacred. The painted rice cake. The sutras. The Jedi texts. That gutted tauntaun Han stuffed Luke inside. All of it from top to bottom, end to end—sacred.

Yoda understood this even if Luke didn't. He panned the Jedi texts as being dull and useless, but he knew they weren't in the tree when he set it afire.

"*Wisdom they held,*" he said of the texts, "*but that library contained nothing that the girl Rey does not already possess.*"

Sly old Jedi Master. That's because Rey *did* possess them. She'd ensconced them in the *Millennium Falcon* not long before Luke went to burn them.

Yoda had no intention of killing the past like Kylo Ren. He knew Rey was the continuation of the Jedi Order, not its destruction. She would build on what came before and take it further than it had ever been.

"That's all very interesting," C-3PO says in a careful tone, "but R2 would like to know what happened to Hsian."

"I'm glad he asked. Now listen to this and tell me if it doesn't remind you of someone."

> After leaving the monastery, Hsian took up residence in the ruins of an abandoned temple. He dressed in tattered robes and established a daily routine that didn't keep him all that busy. One day while he was sweeping the temple grounds, his broom struck a pebble, sending it caroming

off bamboo. When Hsian heard the sound of the pebble hit the bamboo, he realized the "answer" to his master's question and was enlightened. Hsian "saw" his Original Face without the filter of concepts and book learning.

Whether Luke was enlightened by his talk with Yoda or the bonk the little Jedi spirit administered to his head, I don't know for certain. But it's clear Yoda got through to him to some degree. Luke saw "the need in front of his nose" and knew he had to do something to help Leia, Rey, and the Resistance.

With the decision made, Luke overcame his regret and shame for failing Ben. A legend was needed to reignite the rebellion, and Luke stepped forward with what Rey called *"peace and purpose"* to provide a new hope for the galaxy. He confronted Kylo, not as a "great warrior" like he once imagined Yoda to be, but as the man he'd been when he threw aside his lightsaber and refused to kill his father. Nonviolence and compassion were the weapons Luke used then and they were the same ones he brought to bear against his nephew. The hero we remember from Endor harnessed the Force and projected a representation of himself across the galaxy—not to "fight what he hated," to paraphrase Rose Tico, "but to save what he loved."

"Now that I think about it, maybe Luke did realize the wisdom Dogen was saying about sacred texts," I say to C-3PO and R2-D2. "After all, wasn't his Force-projection like a painted picture—an artful representation of himself as real on Crait as Luke was meditating back on Ahch-To?"

Anthony raises his C-3PO mask and says, "Real or painted, I wish I could Force-project up a bit of kidney pie. I'm famished. Oh look, people are standing up. They'll be opening the doors straight away."

Good. That will give me just enough time to talk about a little poem I like.

"A poem?"

"Yes, by another rebel monk: Qui-Gon Jinn."

EPISODE XII

CELEBRATING FAILURE

"It will be a hard life. One without reward. Without remorse. Without regret. A path will be placed before you. The choice is yours alone. Do what you think you cannot do. It will be a hard life. But in the end, you will find out who you are."

Qui-Gon Jinn said those words about Anakin when he was still just a boy, but they could just as easily apply to anyone.

Finding out who you are, as you know by now, is at the heart of Zen. We heard how Hsian struggled with his master's question about his true nature, and we've seen Luke Skywalker find his way, lose it, and find it again. Anyone who has seriously given Zen a shot knows that it can be hard. Maybe even harder than the life Qui-Gon described.

I said at the start of this book that *Zen* basically means "meditation" and *zazen* means "sitting meditation." Zazen is kind of like Jedi meditation and kind of not like it. In Star Wars the Jedi meditate on the mysteries of the Force. They try to unravel its secrets, see into the future, and get in touch with people across the galaxy. That's all wonderful stuff, but it's not really how things work in Zen. Zazen isn't so magical. There are no prophesies to be discovered or riddles to be solved. Actually, zazen, and Zen, itself is totally ordinary. That's one reason why it's so hard. In zazen you just sit on the floor and stare at a wall or pay attention to your breath. It's not exactly like flying through hyperspace. It's not even like dusting crops.

But the fact that Zen is ordinary is pretty much the point. The ordinary stuff you do every day—tying shoes, doing homework, salvaging capacitor bearings from downed star destroyers—these are the things that make up your life. And that makes them the most important stuff you'll ever do.

Zen is real life—that thing you're doing right now. Zen doesn't push you to the past or the future, or to desperate friends out in the Bespin system, as Jedi meditation sometimes seems to. Zen points you back to yourself to "find out who you are."

When you sit Zen, you have no choice but to look at yourself. You can try to hide in thoughts and daydreams, but eventually those lose their steam and it will just be you. And when you see yourself—the self-concept you've so carefully cultivated—without filters and distractions, you may be disturbed by what you see. Like when Luke saw his face behind Vader's mask in the dark side cave.

Qui-Gon promised Anakin a life "without remorse, without regret." For most people new to Zen, this is not their experience. They are filled with remorse and regret because of their mistakes and failures. Even Luke Skywalker, Jedi master and legend, struggled mightily with regret and failure. Facing failure in yourself without anywhere to hide can be demoralizing and make some people never want to practice zazen again. But those that stick with it come to view their failures as benefits and discover a Jedi-like strength within themselves they never knew was there.

R2 whistles and buzzes.

"R2 says he can relate," C-3PO interprets. "He has failed many times. I, however, am quite certain I have not."

"Hmm, I remember a certain protocol droid saying, 'Curse my metal body, I wasn't fast enough. It's all my fault.'"

"Oh, my . . . the trash compactor. Well . . . that hardly counts. Master Luke and the others escaped unharmed."

We've all failed, but not everyone's slip-ups make it to the big screen.

R2 lost his way on Tatooine and was ambushed by Jawas. He was captured by super battle droids and failed to save Anakin and Obi-Wan on the Invisible Hand. He turned on the thermal heater in Leia's Echo Base quarters and soaked all her clothes.

For all R2's successes, he had as many or more failures. And that's perfectly right, isn't it? What is failure, if not a step to success? Many people think of failure as a conclusion, the depressing finale at the end of a quest, but really it's just a pothole in the road. The journey continues after you've tripped. And when you find success along the path—like joining a criminal gang (Han Solo's lifelong wish fulfilled!)—your next step puts your head in a noose when you dump a cargo of refined coaxium. And that failure leads to success on Kessel, which leads to failure on Savareen, which leads to success in a now legendary game of sabaac. And on and on and on.

Failure is just part of the game. There's no reason to let it ruin the fun.

R2 makes a series of beeps.

"He says failure is personal. One chooses to fail," C-3PO informs me.

"Uh, yeah . . . I think I understand, R2. You're *not* saying I choose to fail a test or crash my X-wing into the swamp. But I do choose to call those things failures. Failure is when things don't work out the way I want them to. So, the difference between success and failure or failure and something neutral is my point of view."

R2 bleeps and I don't need C-3PO to tell me he agrees.

Maybe we feel bad about failure because we're looking at everything the wrong way. We're putting too much emphasis on ourselves and our small personal concerns and not enough emphasis on the great big reality we are part of. Kind of like Luke after his little misunderstanding with Ben Solo.

Even years after the incident, he was still stuck in the past and unable to let go of what he had done wrong.

"Still looking to the horizon," Yoda said of him, scolding Luke for failing to be here and now, and for being hung up on the past at the expense of those who needed his help in the present. Then Yoda defied his ghostly limitations and amazingly bonked Luke on the forehead with

his cane. While this was a shocking display of postmortem Jedi powers, it was also a not-so-subtle reminder to his once-and-current student to pay attention to *"the need in front of your nose."*

Justifiably admonished, Luke admitted he had acted unwisely as even the best of us do from time to time (or even daily!). He had allowed his failure with Ben Solo to consume him and subsequently lost sight of what was important—the immediate need to help Rey, Leia, and the floundering Resistance.

"Lost Ben Solo, you did. Lose Rey, we must not," Yoda asserts.

But still Luke is insecure, hesitant—even anxious. Because he let down Ben Solo he believed he could not be what Rey needed him to be.

"Heeded my words not, did you?" Yoda tells him. *"Pass on what you have learned."*

Strength and mastery are all well and good, Yoda says, but weakness, folly, and failure are also crucial. In fact, they are an indispensable element of growth, discovery, success, and happiness.

"Yes, failure most of all," Yoda emphasized to Luke. *"The greatest teacher, failure is."*

Luke wanted to pass on only his successes. He believed there was no value in failure. And yet he placed his failure with Ben above everything else. So much so that he exiled himself to a distant island and cut himself off from the Force. Luke blamed himself too much for his own mistakes and took too much responsibility for the shortcomings of the Jedi Order.

Your failures are not yours. The person you are at this moment is completely different from the person who messed up in the past. The person here and now is not at fault. But that person—you right now—*is* responsible. You are responsible for what your past self did but not to blame for it.

It is the blame, the guilt, the remorse that weighs us down. We can let go of all that. We can unburden the regret and still take responsibility and make amends for past wrongdoing. It took a visit from Yoda and a bonk on the head to make Luke finally accept this truth.

"Look, sir," C-3PO cuts in. "People are standing. It appears the Star Wars Celebration staff will be allowing us to enter at any moment."

"I better hurry this up, then."

Qui-Gon said, *"A path will be placed before you. The choice is yours alone. Do what you think you cannot do."*

The one thing you are truly responsible for is what you do. Your actions, your choices, the path you take at this moment carries over to the next. Be kind to your future self. Do today what you will appreciate tomorrow. And whatever you do, do it wholeheartedly, like Bodhidharma taught. Do it with your entire body and mind. Your life is so brief. It is here now and gone like that. Don't let it slip away in forgetfulness.

And also please remember that what you do matters. What you do creates our shared existence. What you do shapes your mind and your experience and colors your entire life. If Dogen is right and we are paintings painting paintings, make sure yours is a masterpiece.

The sound of the Star Wars "Main Title" theme suddenly bursts into my ears and a roar of excitement erupts from the crowd. Star Wars Celebration has finally begun.

I hastily close my laptop and stuff it into my backpack. I stand up thinking about my choices, my regrets, and how hard life can be, like Qui-Gon said. Then something bumps my leg. It is R2 or Kenny or both or neither.

Somehow the fan-made droid emits an image from its holoprojector. It is a hologram of the picture of Bodhidharma I showed him. In true Zen paradoxical fashion, Bodhidharma winks at me with a lidless eye. His dour lips curve into a slight smile. And I hear his unspoken message.

Life may sometimes be hard. You may make mistakes you regret. But every moment, every experience, every feeling is the entire universe in disguise. The awakened mind sees its totality and celebrates it all like it is complete victory.

The line moves, and I step forward to celebrate Star Wars and every up and down of this miraculous gift of life I have received.

THE PADAWAN HANDBOOK:
ZEN PARABLES FOR THE WOULD-BE JEDI

PARABLES ON WORTHY CONDUCT

O Apprentice, the way of mindfulness is a difficult one. Commit yourself completely. Always remain diligent because the path of practice is narrow and continuously assailed by the energies of the dark side.

Who is better protected: a Jedi with a legion of his fellow Knights at his side, surrounded by a squadron of battle tanks and ground assault vehicles, or one who conducts himself with honesty and kindness, whose behavior is upright, and whose thoughts are lovingly directed toward all

From *The Dharma of Star Wars.*

beings? Clearly, one who conducts himself with honesty and kindness, whose behavior is upright, and whose thoughts are lovingly directed toward all beings is better protected because he has guarded himself against the internal armies of the dark side that assail his mind.

Apprentice, it is best not to speak, to tell others how they should live; let your life be your teaching.

Self-pride is a complex that eats the heart and mind of all, including the Jedi. If you think you are greater than other beings, equal to other beings, or less than other beings you have succumbed to self-pride. Guard against these three complexes night and day.

The greatest of all Jedi are not the ones who defeat a thousand opponents; they are the ones who triumph over themselves. Without patience one cannot truly call himself a student of the Way. Develop your patience—make impulse and whim as uncommon to you as honesty and morality are to a Hutt.

Do not abandon the Sith. Do not close your eyes to the Night Sisters. Commit yourself to finding ways to be with those who are gripped by the dark side, so that you can understand their situation deeply and help relieve them of their anguish.

Be an inspiration to your fellow Jedi. Carry yourself with grace and kindness. Do not allow arrogance to distinguish you like fools in martial attire, draped with emblems and medals. A Jedi should wear the simple cloak of his order with humility. When those who avoid the Way, pursuing only what is pleasant, attached to the senses, see one conducted so, they will experience their loss and lament their ways.

Young pupil, always remember:
Where there is anger, offer kindness.
Where there is selfishness, offer generosity.
Where there is despair, offer hope.
Where there are lies, offer truth.
Where there is injury, offer forgiveness.
Where there is sorrow, offer joy.
Where there is hatred, offer love.
Where there is evil, offer goodness.

PARABLES ON ATTACHMENT AND DESIRE

Beware of the binding tractor-beam of attachment. For beings attached to their bodies, thoughts, feelings, beliefs, perceptions, or consciousness are imprisoned and can never know true freedom.

To commit to the Way is to give up selfish desires and to live for the benefit of all beings, Gungans, Jedi, and Sith.

Jedi, the joy that arises with bodily pleasure offers fleeting benefits and little sweetness. It is fruit that quickly becomes bitter and over time poisons the one who eats it. The joy that arises with equanimity, that is free from attachment to sensual desires, is sweet and nourishing. Its benefits are profound and ever present. Look carefully, young one, at the objects you desire. Are they truly what you believe them to be? What resides in them that does not reside everywhere? What do they hold that cannot be found in every element of the galaxy?

Ambition and desire lead to the dark side. Be wise, my determined apprentice, there is no happiness like the happiness of having few desires.

PARABLES ON COMPASSION

A Jedi who is worthy keeps compassion foremost in his thoughts. His compassion extends to all beings in the galaxy. With an open and loving heart he directs these thoughts for their universal benefit:

> May terrestrial beings, arboreal beings, beings of the skies, beings of the seas and oceans, beings of the stars and asteroids, beings visible and invisible, beings living and yet to live, all dwell in a state of bliss, free from injury and sorrow, tranquil and contented. May no one harm another, deceive another, oppress another, or put another in danger. May all beings love and protect each other just as a master loves and

protects his Padawan. May boundless love pervade the entire galaxy.

PARABLES ON IMPERMANENCE

The eyes are the tools of deception that conjure the illusion of death. Look! See! There is no death, young one, except that which exists in the mind shrouded by the dark side.

Remember, young Jedi: death lurks around every corner, and it cannot be bargained with. Knowing this, if you are wise, you will put aside all quarrels.

Life is precious to all beings. All beings fear death. Knowing this, my young apprentice, and caring for others as you care for yourself, do not be eager to deal out death.

The Sith cannot escape death. Death, not just of the corporeal body, but of all manifestations of the mind, is inevitable. It is the way of all things, the way of the Force.

When someone is dying of thirst it is too late to dig a well. If you wait until you are upon your deathbed to practice the Way it will be too late. Death will not wait a moment longer than it is ready. Do not be lazy, Padawan; be steadfast as Master Windu.

Life is impermanence. All things are subject to change, and nothing can last forever. Look at your hand, young one, and ask yourself, "Whose hand is this?" Can your hand correctly be called "yours"? Or is it the hand of your mother, the hand of your father? The hand of a senator, the hand of a Jedi? Reflect on the impermanent nature of your hand, the hand with which you once battled a Nexu on Geonosis.

PARABLES ON THE DARK SIDE

A Jedi who is ruled by anger, by hatred, by jealousy, by desire is bound to the dark side just as a mynock binds itself to power cables.

A Jedi who harbors resentment and holds on to the thought "That person was cruel to me and showed me no respect" nourishes the dark side in himself. A Jedi who lets go of resentment and releases pride uproots hatred from himself.

Ignorance is the path to the dark side. One who is practicing the Way must always keep the mind open. Such a one must observe, listen, and learn. The Truth is found in the most unlikely of places.

Like biker-scouts at the head of an army, thought is the vanguard of all action. If your thoughts are influenced by the dark side, your actions will be evil. Observe your thoughts carefully, for they may be leading you down the path of the dark side.

Anger is a powerful emotion of the dark side. It can destroy harmony and lead to argument, conflict, and even death. When anger arises in you do not give in to it. Remain mindful, observing the anger, but not acting upon it. If you believe someone else is the cause of your anger, look again. They are a mirror reflecting your own mind.

Hatred cannot defeat hatred, young Jedi. If hatred is directed toward you, combat it with kindness. That is the only way to defeat hatred.

PARABLES ON WISE ACTION

Before you act, young one, you must reflect. Reflect unwisely and troubles follow as surely as a droid follows the mandates of his programming. Reflect wisely and troubles are like a shadow in the void of space, unseen and unfelt.

When putting on your robes, igniting your lightsaber, or using the Jedi Mind Trick—when acting in any way—always ask yourself: "Does this action support my true happiness and the true happiness of others? Does this action support my aspiration to transform the energies of the dark side within me?" If so, then you may be sure your action is worthy of the Way.

Thoughts are like tractor-beams that pull you off course. When you act, act! There is no room for thought.

O Apprentice, you inherit the results of your actions in body, speech, and mind. The ground you stand on today was produced by your actions of yesterday. Actions of worthy conduct produce a stable foundation as firm as permacreate. Unworthy actions produce an unstable path sure to slope into a sarlaac.

Parables on the Mind

Hold the mind like a cup of water in the hand—still and calm. Like the Force, let thoughts flow through you. Close your hand and you lose yourself.

If you are not aware of your mind, young one, you cannot know it. If you do not know your mind, you cannot care for it. If you do not care for your mind, you cannot nourish it and grow in wisdom.

O Learner, you must tame the mind like a handler tames a reek. As an untamed reek can bite and gore so too can the untamed mind destroy you.

The blade of a lightsaber is only as good as its crystal. If the crystal is impure, poorly cut, and fractured, the blade will be dangerous and poor. If, on the other hand, the crystal is pure, well cut, and not fractured, the blade is safe and good. The same is true with the mind. If the mind is impure, poorly trained, and unfocused, the resultant life will be dangerous and poor. But a pure mind, well trained and focused, will bring about a life that is both safe and good.

O Apprentice, you must recognize and abandon the impurities of your mind, the impurities of anger, hatred, aggression, fear, despair, avarice, superfluous desire, obstinacy, arrogance, and jealousy. When you are able to abandon the afflictions of the mind, you will find serenity and happiness.

PARABLES ON MINDFULNESS

Whether sitting, standing, walking, or lying down, be mindful day and night of your bodily position and actions. Whether pleasant, neutral, or unpleasant, be mindful day and night of your feelings. Whether kind, impartial, or cruel, be mindful day and night of your thoughts. Whether focused, ambivalent, or dispersed, be mindful day and night of your state of mind.

Dwelling in meditation, the mind is at peace—emotions rise like a hungry gooba fish; left alone they cannot disturb the surface.

Harmony arises when there is balance. Balance arises when there is equanimity. Equanimity is the fruit of mindfulness and patience. Take your time, young one, perform every action with complete awareness, and harmony will be your reward.

Attention to the moment reveals what is hidden. With mindfulness of the living Force it is possible to know what is unknown. Focus on what you are doing. Concentration should be fully directed on the object of your inquiry, the object of your task, like the beam of an ion cannon is focused on its target.

A Youngling found a holocron and spoke to a distant master. "I've heard the Way is a doctrine of awakening," the fledgling Jedi said. "What is your method?"

Through the holocron, the master replied, "We walk, we eat, we wash, we sit…"

"What kind of method is that? Everyone walks, eats, washes, and sits."

"Child, when we walk we are aware we are walking. When we eat we are aware we are eating. When others walk, eat, wash, or sit down, they are generally not aware of what they are doing."

PARABLES ON TIME

Always in motion the future is; it is unborn, unsubstantial. It is merely an image, like a hologram of a living being. We can no more touch and feel the future than we can touch and feel a hologram. The future, then, is unreal because it is not present. Only the present is real; only this moment is alive.

When considering the past or the future, dear Apprentice, be mindful of the present. If, while considering the past, you identify with the past, become caught in the past, and burdened by the past, then you have abandoned reality as Count Dooku abandoned his brethren. If, while considering the future, you identify with the future, become caught in the future, and are burdened by the future, then you have chased illusions as the Sith chase their dream of immortality. Conversely, when considering the past, if you do not identify with the past, or become caught or burdened by the past, then you, like a once-careless Jedi finding your misplaced lightsaber, have not lost yourself in the past. And if, when considering the future, you do not identify with the future, or become caught or burdened by the future, then, like a Jedi turning away from the dark side, you have not lost yourself in the future.

Parables on Wisdom

The true weapon is the lightsaber of wisdom, which cuts the bonds of ignorance from our mind.

A Jedi ought to choose his words carefully and intelligently. A single word of wisdom says more than a thousand words spoken idly. Thoroughly listen and reflect. The words you utter can have a profound impact on the listener. Will they bring peace or will they cause harm?

I heard these words of a Jedi master one time: Wisdom exists when you understand something and recognize that you understand it and when you do not understand something and you recognize that you do not understand it.

Padawan, do not cling to views or bind yourself to ideology. The knowledge you now have is not changeless, absolute truth. Truth is found in life and is continuously learned and relearned. Be open to the experiences and insights of others; do not remain fixed to a single point of view. The Way of the Jedi is to put aside dogma and touch the truth present here and now in the living Force.

Release all holds on doctrine or dogma, even Jedi ones, and you will be counted among the wise.

About the Author

The author as a child, age five, dressed for Halloween.

Matthew Bortolin wears his personally made Jedi robes and lightsaber when he attends Star Wars Celebration, as he has to many Star Wars movies (including *The Clone Wars*). He has talked about the links between Star Wars and Zen with CNN, *Newsweek*, *USA Today*, *Good Morning America*, and several online magazines and fan websites. He was ordained by Thich Nhat Hanh into the Zen community and is the author of *The Dharma of Star Wars*. He lives in Ventura, California.

What to read next from Wisdom Publications

The Dharma of Star Wars
Matthew Bortolin

"With humor, strong examples, and timeless wisdom, Bortolin offers a new way to think about a pop culture phenomenon. Lead us to Yoda, he does."
—*Publishers Weekly*

Saltwater Buddha
A Surfer's Quest to Find Zen on the Sea
Jaimal Yogis

"Heartfelt, honest, and deceptively simple. It's great stuff with the words 'cult classic' stamped all over it."
—Alex Wade, author of *Surf Nation*

Hardcore Zen
Punk Rock, Monster Movies, and the Truth About Reality
Brad Warner

"*Hardcore Zen* is to Buddhism what the Ramones were to rock and roll: A clear-cut, no-bulls**t offering of truth."
—Miguel Chen, Teenage Bottlerocket

Buddhism for Dudes
A Jarhead's Field Guide to Mindfulness
Gerry Stribling

"*Buddhism for Dudes* shoots straight and doesn't blink. It's John Wayne meets Zen, complete with all the wisdom and tough-guy charm you'd expect."
—Matthew Bortolin, author of *The Dharma of Star Wars*

Novice to Master
An Ongoing Lesson in the Extent of My Own Stupidity
Sōkō Morinaga
Translated by Belenda Attaway Yamakawa

"This wise and warm book should be read by all."
—Anthony Swofford, author of *Jarhead*

The Fool's Guide to Actual Happiness
Mark Van Buren

"This dude really gets it! The Buddha believed in happiness for everyone, and Van Buren gets you there in this concise and simple book that's just loaded with wisdom."
—Gerry Stribling, author of *Buddhism for Dudes*

About Wisdom Publications

Wisdom Publications is the leading publisher of classic and contemporary Buddhist books and practical works on mindfulness. To learn more about us or to explore our other books, please visit our website at wisdomexperience.org or contact us at the address below.

Wisdom Publications
199 Elm Street
Somerville, MA 02144 USA

We are a 501(c)(3) organization, and donations in support of our mission are tax deductible.

Wisdom Publications is affiliated with the Foundation for the Preservation of the Mahayana Tradition (FPMT).